The Best of
IRISH COUNTRY COOKING

TRADITIONAL AND CONTEMPORARY RECIPES

FOR LOUIS, EVA,
AND CHRISTINE

NUALA CULLEN

The Best of
IRISH COUNTRY COOKING

TRADITIONAL AND CONTEMPORARY RECIPES

Interlink Books

An imprint of Interlink Publishing Group, Inc.
Northampton, Massachusetts

CONTENTS

Bluebells bloom in spring at Killarney National Park in County Kerry.

INTRODUCTION

The vision of ancient Celtic Ireland that has come down to us through folklore and poetry is of a land of plenty, where poetry and music were among the important occupations of the people, and honor and hospitality went hand in hand.

Through the centuries, hospitality continued to be a matter of pride for rich and poor alike. Nearer to our own times, in the eighteenth and nineteenth centuries, successive travelers to Ireland invariably commented on the lavish welcome, the rich variety and quantity of food, and the large numbers of persons entertained. The ill-fated dependence upon the potato by almost one-quarter of the population, however, and the tragic aftermath of the failure of the potato crop in the successive famines of the 1840s, is all too well known. Life changed profoundly for many people as a consequence, and the tradition of prodigal hospitality was almost swept away.

Ireland, however, is a natural food-producing country and, in recent decades, extensive research has yielded an improved understanding of the best production methods for our food resources, creating a true land of plenty. Irish products are now in demand all over Europe. There has been a renaissance in Irish cooking, too: a new generation of Irish chefs, cosmopolitan in their training though with roots in their own tradition, are creating a discernibly Irish style of cooking that allows the excellent raw materials to speak for themselves. We are also fortunate that many of the festival days are still observed in Ireland, even if only in perfunctory way. Such feast days obviously put the emphasis on seasonal ingredients. The recipes included in this book aim to give an idea of some of the dishes that have been in common use in Ireland for many hundreds of years, with a few exceptions.

I hope that you will enjoy them and that they will contribute in some measure to the enjoyment of your guests and the conviviality of the dinner table, a pleasure as important in Ireland today as it has been for centuries.

The rolling hills of County Kerry.

APPETIZERS

MUSSELS WITH BACON AND RED WINE

SERVES 6 AS AN APPETIZER OR 4 AS A MAIN COURSE

"Lord Smart (to Neverout): Tom, they say fish should swim thrice.

Neverout: How is that, my Lord?

Lord Smart: Why, Tom, first it should swim in the Sea (Do you mind me?), then it should swim in Butter; and at last Sirrah, it should swim in good Claret."
Jonathan Swift, Polite Conversation

8½ cups/3 lb live mussels

1 cup/240 ml red wine

2 tablespoons butter

1 fresh thyme sprig

6 streaky bacon strips, chopped

4 shallots

2 garlic cloves, finely chopped

3 large ripe tomatoes, de-seeded and chopped

1 tablespoon all-purpose flour

2 tablespoons chopped fresh flat-leaved parsley, plus extra to garnish

salt and freshly ground black pepper

fresh crusty bread, to serve

Clean the mussels thoroughly, discarding any that are broken or that don't close when sharply tapped, and put them in a large saucepan with the wine. Cover, bring to a boil, and cook for 2 minutes, shaking the pan from time to time, until the mussels are open. Transfer the mussels to a bowl, discarding any that do not open. Strain the liquid carefully into a bowl, discarding any sand or grit.

Melt 1 tablespoon butter in a saucepan, add the thyme and bacon, and cook until crisp. Then add the shallots and garlic and cook until soft. Add the tomatoes.

Blend the remaining butter and the flour together and stir into the saucepan, a little at a time, stirring until the flour is cooked and the sauce is smooth. Add the mussel liquid gradually, stirring until the sauce has thickened. If it is too thick, add a little water. Reheat the mussels in the sauce for a few moments, then stir in the parsley. Check and adjust the seasoning. Garnish with parsley and serve with fresh crusty bread.

Previous Page: Fishing boats at Dingle Peninsula in Lough Gill, County Kerry.

SOUSED HERRINGS

SERVES 4

The herring was once a staple of the Irish diet, and its seasonal reappearance was greeted with pleasure by rich and poor alike. Sousing, a simple way of preserving fish, became very popular in its own right. The sousing liquid here is a mild one, so if you like your herrings spicy, leave them in the cold marinade for a few hours before cooking to develop the flavors.

8–10 herring fillets

8–10 shallots

2–3 bay leaves

1 onion, finely sliced

1 tablespoon chopped fresh parsley

boiled baby potatoes, to serve

FOR THE MARINADE

1¼ cups/300 ml hard cider or white-wine vinegar

1¼ cups/300 ml dry hard cider or white wine

2 teaspoons juniper berries, slightly crushed

½ tsp chili powder or chopped fresh chilies, or to taste

1–2 tablespoons each of brown sugar, mustard seeds, and black peppercorns

Boil the marinade ingredients together gently for a few minutes. Cool and allow to infuse for 30 minutes.

Preheat the oven to 300°F/150°C. Lay out the fish fillets on a board and arrange a peeled shallot and a bay leaf on each one. Roll up and secure with a cocktail stick. Arrange in an ovenproof dish, scatter the onion slices over the top, and pour the marinade into the dish. Cover with foil and bake for 30–40 minutes.

Garnish with the parsley and serve with the boiled potatoes. To serve cold, cool and pack the fish into a plastic container small enough to allow the cooking liquid to cover them entirely, and chill, overnight if possible. Serve with pickles or pickled onions with mustard or horseradish sauce on the side. They will keep for 2–3 days in the fridge.

COD ROE AND COD ROE PÂTÉ

SERVES 4 AS AN APPETIZER OR 2 AS A LUNCH DISH

The season for cod roe is very short, a mere 2–3 weeks between February and March, so it is important to make the most of it. Roe freezes well, either raw or cooked, so it's a good idea to buy extra when it is available. Smaller eggs are more delicate in texture, but the larger ones are very good, too.

To cook, simply tie the roe loosely in a plastic bag, cover with boiling water, and simmer slowly until firm to the touch. Leave to cool and remove from the bag. The simplest and most traditional preparation is to cut it into thick slices, dip in seasoned flour, or egg and breadcrumbs, and fry gently in a mixture of butter and oil until crisp. It is delicious for breakfast, with crisp bacon and roasted tomatoes or mushrooms, or for lunch with creamy mashed potatoes and a slice of lemon.

FOR THE PÂTÉ

4–5 oz /110–140 g cooked cod roe

4–6 tablespoons /55–75 g butter, melted

juice and grated zest of ½ lemon

1 tablespoon chopped fresh chives

salt

cayenne or chili pepper to taste

Purée all the ingredients in a food processor until smooth, seasoning with salt and cayenne or chili pepper to taste. Pack into individual ramekins and chill. This is delicious served with hot toast as an appetizer. If it's not to be eaten for a few hours, cover with melted butter before chilling.

Opposite: *Reaching for Ireland's favorite drink.*

OYSTERS WITH SPICY PORK PATTIES

SERVES 2

St. Valentine's Day calls for something special: delicious, of course, with amorous associations, and not too much trouble. The old fashion of eating chilled oysters and chipolatas (thin, spicy sausages) with champagne or white wine seems ideal. Chipolatas can be hard to find, so prepare and chill your own pork patties the day before and then cook them up quickly.

½ onion, finely chopped

1 garlic clove

2 tablespoons/30 g butter

¾ lb/350 g lean pork, finely ground

2 teaspoons Yorkshire relish or Worcestershire sauce

a pinch each of dried thyme, grated nutmeg, and hot chili powder

1 tablespoon finely chopped fresh parsley

12 oysters, opened (see note), on the deep half of the shell

Cook the onion and garlic in a little of the butter until soft. (If you are making the patties in advance, cool the onion mixture, and chill until required.)

Mix the meat with the remaining butter, the relish or sauce, and the seasonings and herbs, then stir in the onion and garlic and mix thoroughly. The mixture should be hot and spicy but not so the finished patties kill the taste of the oysters and wine. With floured hands, shape the mixture into small patties, about 1 ½ inches/4 cm wide. Cook them in a frying pan, without any extra fat, for about 10 minutes, flipping them over halfway through cooking.

Serve hot, alternating with the chilled oysters.

Note: to open an oyster, hold it firmly in your left hand and insert a short, sharp knife near the hinge, working it from right to left until it begins to release; then pry it open.

POTTED SALMON

SERVES 6 AS AN APPETIZER OR 4 AS A MAIN COURSE

This eighteenth-century Irish recipe, from an old family cookbook, uses ginger, mace, lemon zest, and bay leaves. There are no exact measurements. The spices can be adjusted to taste and the quantity of fish available, but the initial salting should be generous. It is delicious as a light lunch for 3 or 4 or, potted in ramekins, it will serve 6 as an appetizer. Serve with some good bread, triangles of hot toast, or crackers.

1 lb/450 g salmon, deboned and skin removed
2 tablespoons sea salt
1 teaspoon ground mace
a pinch of ground ginger
grated zest of 1 lemon
1 bay leaf
1 stick/110 g butter, clarified (see note below)
bread, toast, or crackers, to serve

Preheat the oven to 300°F/150°C. Cut the fish into several pieces. Rub all the surfaces well with salt and set aside for 3 hours.

Scrape the salt from the fish and wipe it with paper towel, but don't wash it. Mix together the spices and lemon zest and rub into the fish. Pack the fish into a 2½ cup/600 ml oven dish, with the bay leaf on top, and cover with foil. Bake for about 20–30 minutes, or until the fish is cooked. Pour off the juices and remove the bay leaf; then fill the dish with clarified butter, covering the fish completely. Keep for a day or two before using. To keep for a longer period (up to 6–7 days), fill the butter up to a depth of ½ inch/1 cm over the top of the fish. Store, well-covered, in the fridge.

Note: To clarify butter, melt the butter gently, then allow it to stand until the sediment falls to the bottom. Carefully pour the clear butter over the fish, leaving the sediment behind.

SMOKED SALMON PÂTÉ

SERVES 6

12 oz/350 g smoked salmon
¾ cup/175 g crème fraîche
grated zest and juice of ½ lemon
fresh dill sprigs
6 tablespoons/75 g butter, melted
½ cup/125 ml heavy cream

TO DECORATE
small fresh dill sprigs
pickles

Skin and chop the salmon, removing any bones or hard pieces. Place it in a food processor with the crème fraîche, lemon zest and juice, a few sprigs of dill, and 4 tablespoons/55 g of the melted butter. Pulse until it is your preferred texture, and then, by hand, gradually beat in the cream.

Rub one large or six little ramekins with oil and pack in the pâté. Brush the top with the remaining butter, cover, and chill. To serve, decorate with dill and pickles. Serve with hot toast or crackers.

SCOTCH EGGS

SERVES 8 AS AN APPETIZER OR 4 AS A MAIN COURSE

In spite of the name, this combination of pork and eggs has a long and happy history in Ireland. Back in fashion now, they are still in demand for parties and picnics. The mustard mayonnaise really lifts the flavor. Served hot, they're great for lunch or supper too, especially with good buttery mashed potatoes. Allow one per person, with a few extra. They won't go to waste.

4 eggs

3 scallions, chopped

2 tablespoons/30 g butter

7 oz/200 g very finely ground pork or good sausage meat

1 tablespoon cornstarch

1 tablespoon Worcestershire sauce or soy sauce

1 tablespoon lemon juice

salt and freshly ground black pepper

1 egg yolk

2–3 tablespoons all-purpose flour, for dusting

oil, for deep-frying

crisp lettuce, to serve

FOR THE MUSTARD MAYONNAISE

2 egg yolks, at room temperature

1 tablespoon mild Dijon mustard

1¼ cups/300 ml olive oil

salt

about 1 tablespoon horseradish cream sauce

Put the eggs into boiling water and cook for 10 minutes exactly, then plunge into cold water to cool.

In a small pan, cook the chopped scallions in the butter until soft. Allow to cool. Mix the pork, scallions, cornstarch, Worcestershire or soy sauce, lemon juice, and salt and pepper together to make a paste. Shell the eggs and dry them carefully. Roll in egg yolk, then in flour, shaking off any excess.

Divide the pork into 4 portions and, with floured hands, shape around each egg, encasing them completely. Deep-fry the eggs in sufficient oil to cover, turning frequently to prevent splitting, for about 6–8 minutes until golden brown. Drain on paper towel.

For an appetizer, slice the eggs lengthways and arrange on crisp lettuce. For a picnic, leave them whole.

To make the mustard mayonnaise, beat the egg yolks with the mustard, then slowly pour in the oil, drop by drop at first, and then in a thin stream as it begins to emulsify, stirring continuously, or use an electric beater on medium speed. Season well with a pinch of salt and add the horseradish cream sauce to taste.

Note: should the mayonnaise separate, start again with another egg yolk in a clean bowl and add the mixture, drop by drop, as before.

DEVILED SHRIMP

SERVES 4 AS AN APPETIZER OR 2 AS A MAIN COURSE

"Devils"—highly spiced morsels of fish or fowl—were hugely popular in Ireland in the past, after dinner, when they were considered a stimulant to the punch bowl, or before dinner, as a spur to jaded appetites. There was great competition for the definitive "devil" and recipes were constantly exchanged, many of tear-compelling pungency.

12 large raw shrimp in their shells

1 teaspoon sea salt

1 teaspoon cayenne pepper

1 teaspoon paprika

1 teaspoon ground cumin

2 limes or 1 lemon

2 tablespoons melted butter

chili powder to taste

Peel the body shells from the shrimp, but leave the tails intact.

To make the "devil," mix the salt and spices together and form into a paste with the melted butter, the zest of 1 lime or ½ lemon, and a little juice. To make it hotter, add more cayenne or chilli, but taste constantly. Marinate the shrimp in this mixture for a couple of hours in the fridge.

Grill or broil the shrimp on medium heat, turning regularly, until they are just opaque and the tail shells are pink. Slice the remaining lime or lemon and serve the shrimp garnished with the citrus slices.

Note: if cooked shrimp are used, grill or broil them just enough to heat them through thoroughly.

SMOKED SALMON TARTLETS

SERVES 6

*These delicate little tartlets, filled with smoked salmon mousse,
can be garnished with whatever suits your taste. Try slivers of anchovies
with capers, halved quails eggs, or sprigs of fresh dill.*

FOR THE PASTRY

2 cups/10 oz/280 g all-purpose flour

salt

½ teaspoon grated lemon zest

10 tablespoons/140 g butter

1 egg yolk

1 tablespoon very cold water

FOR THE FILLING

½ lb/225 g smoked salmon

1 cup/240 ml crème fraîche or heavy cream,
    or a mixture

2 teaspoons finely chopped fresh dill or tarragon
    or ½ teaspoon dried

½ teaspoon paprika

2 teaspoons lemon juice

1 teaspoon grated lemon zest

a dash of Tabasco or chili sauce

fresh chervil, tarragon, or dill leaves, to garnish

TO SERVE

oil and balsamic vinegar, to taste

mixed salad leaves

To make the pastry, sift the flour with a pinch of salt and stir in the lemon zest. Rub in the butter until the mixture resembles breadcrumbs. Moisten with the egg yolk and the tablespoon of cold water and mix to a soft dough. Wrap in plastic wrap and chill for half an hour.

Preheat the oven to 375°F/190°C. Roll out the pastry to fit six 3 inch/8 cm buttered tartlet pans. Prick the pastry bottoms. Line with parchment paper and then fit the pans into each other, putting an empty pan (or foil and dried beans) into the top one. Bake for 15 minutes. Remove from the oven, separate the pans, and put back in the oven for a further 4–5 minutes or so until crisp but not too brown. These can be made in advance and kept in the pans. Don't fill them, however, until shortly before serving, so they remain crisp.

Put the salmon and crème fraîche or cream in a food processor with the herbs, paprika, lemon juice and zest, and a dash of Tabasco or chili sauce. Taste for flavor. Process until a stiff purée is formed and add a little more cream if it's too stiff. Chill until required. Divide the filling between the pastry shells and arrange the garnish on top.

Whisk together the oil and vinegar to make the dressing. Arrange some salad leaves on each plate and place a tart beside the leaves. Sprinkle a few drops of dressing over the leaves and around the plate.

MUSHROOMS IN PASTRY

SERVES 8 AS AN APPETIZER OR 4 AS A MAIN COURSE

There is a charm in mushrooms that is never quite dispelled by familiarity. Use as many kinds as you can find; their different flavors blend together subtly.

½ lb/225 g spinach

4-6 tablespoons/55-75 g butter

1 garlic clove, finely chopped

1 lb/450 g mixed mushrooms

1 tablespoon mushroom ketchup
    or Worcestershire sauce

salt and freshly ground black pepper

½ teaspoon cayenne pepper

1 lb/450 g frozen or homemade puff pastry

1 egg, beaten

generous ½ cup/150 ml cream

Preheat the oven to 375°F/190°C. Wash and coarsely chop the spinach. Melt a pat of butter in a large frying pan and gently cook the garlic for a few moments, and then add the spinach and toss until it is slightly wilted. Remove the spinach from the pan and squeeze out any juices back into the pan.

Wipe and trim the mushrooms and chop them coarsely. Add a tablespoon of butter and one tablespoon of ketchup or Worcestershire sauce to the pan and cook the mushrooms until they are reduced but still juicy (if using oyster mushrooms, don't put them in until the last moment). Season well with salt, pepper, and cayenne. Remove the mushrooms to cool, but leave the juices in the pan.

Roll out the pastry into 2 rectangles about 10 x 8 inches/25 x 20 cm and leave to rest for 10 minutes. Grease a baking sheet and cover with a sheet of parchment paper. Place one sheet of the pastry on top of the baking sheet and cover with the spinach, leaving a ½ inch/1 cm space around the edges. Pile the mushrooms on top of the spinach and even them out. Season well and sprinkle with the cayenne. Dot with the remaining butter, then cover with the other rectangle of pastry, press the dampened edges together, and make a vent in the top. Brush with the beaten egg.

Bake until golden, about 40 minutes. Add the cream and remaining butter and bubble for a few minutes to make a sauce.

BLACK PUDDING PATTIES

SERVES 8 AS AN APPETIZER OR 4 AS A LIGHT LUNCH

Black pudding (blood sausage) and white pudding (made without blood) are usually eaten at breakfast. You can find them in Irish specialty stores or online.

¾ lb/350 g Irish black pudding, or other coarse-textured pudding

½ lb/225 g potato, freshly cooked

4 scallions, finely chopped

1 large cooking apple, peeled and grated or finely chopped

4 tablespoons/55 g butter

1 egg, beaten

salt and freshly ground black pepper

1–2 tablespoons milk (optional)

2 tablespoons whole-wheat flour

3 tablespoons oil, for frying

2 large eating apples

small glass of white wine, vermouth, or stock

arugula, watercress, or other leaves, to garnish

Peel the casing from the black pudding and finely crumble it into a mixing bowl. Mash in the potato, the finely chopped scallions, apple, 2 tablespoons/30 g of the butter, the beaten egg, and salt and pepper. Mix well together, then form into 12 patties, adding a tablespoon or so of milk if the mixture is too dry. Dust with the whole-wheat flour and fry gently in the oil until hot and crisp. Keep warm.

Wash the eating apples and cut across into ½ inch/1 cm slices. Stamp out the cores. In a clean pan, fry the apple slices in the remaining butter until beginning to brown but not breaking up. Arrange these on the plates, two per person, and put the patties on top. Deglaze the pan with the wine and pour the juices around the patties. Garnish with the arugula, watercress, or other leaves.

Below: The Conor Pass and Brandon Peak in County Kerry.

OYSTERS IN CHAMPAGNE SAUCE

SERVES 4

The charm of this dish lies in the combination of the hot sauce with the cold oysters, the perfect introduction to the Christmas dinner. The sauce can be made in advance and reheated.

24 oysters

3 shallots, very finely chopped

2 tablespoons/30 g butter

1½ tablespoons all-purpose flour

a glass of champagne or white wine

1¼ cups/300 ml cream

cayenne pepper or hot sauce

chopped fresh parsley, to garnish

1 little gem lettuce, cut into strips

2 lemons, quartered

Scrub the oysters thoroughly and soak them for an hour or so in cold water. Open the oysters carefully (see below), saving as much of their liquid as possible, and put them to chill while you make the sauce. Strain the liquid through a fine sieve.

Cook the shallots and butter in a pan until transparent but not brown. Add the flour and stir well until it's cooked. Add the champagne or wine and the strained oyster liquid to the roux, whisking well to prevent lumps and cooking until reduced somewhat, about 5 or 6 minutes. Gradually add the cream and simmer gently until the sauce has reduced and thickened sufficiently. Season to your taste with the cayenne or hot sauce—it probably won't need salt.

Just before you are ready to serve, arrange the oysters in their shells on plates and put a spoonful of the hot sauce over each cold oyster. Garnish with the parsley, lettuce, and lemon wedges.

Note: to open an oyster, hold it firmly in your left hand and insert a short, sharp knife near the hinge, working it from right to left until the muscle is severed; then pry the oyster open.

SMOKED FISH TART
WITH ARDRAHAN CHEESE

SERVES 6 AS AN APPETIZER OR 4 AS A MAIN COURSE

Combining Ardrahan cheese, from Kanturk, County Cork, with smoked fish is the inspirational idea of Geert Maes, chef patron of Gaby's Restaurant in Killarney, one of Ireland's most respected restaurants. It is partnered here with smoked haddock, to make a simple but delicious tart. Ardrahan cheese is a washed-rind semi-soft cheese, somewhat similar in flavor to Swiss Appenzeller. Look for it in specialty stores or online.

FOR THE PASTRY

1 stick/110 g butter

scant 1 ½ cups/7 oz/200 g all-purpose flour

¼ teaspoon salt

1 egg yolk

1–2 tablespoons very cold water, if necessary

FOR THE FILLING

1 onion, chopped

1 carrot, chopped

½ tablespoon oil

1 bay leaf

a few black peppercorns

½ lb/225 g smoked haddock or cod

4 oz/110 g Ardrahan cheese

4 large eggs

1 ¼ cups/300 ml cream

freshly ground black pepper and grated nutmeg

Preheat the oven to 400°F/200°C. To make the pastry, rub the butter into the sifted flour and salt, moisten with the egg yolk, adding a tablespoon or so of cold water if required to knead gently to a soft dough. Roll out, or press into a 9 x 3 inch /23 x 5 cm quiche pan. Chill until required.

In a sauté pan, gently fry the chopped onion and carrot in the oil until soft, then add the bay leaf and peppercorns and enough water just to cover. Boil for about 10 minutes. Gently poach the fish in this stock until cooked, 5–6 minutes. Take out the fish, flake it, and remove any bones or hard pieces. Strain the stock and keep it for soups.

With a potato peeler, remove the thin outer rind from the Ardrahan cheese and then cut the cheese into thin slices. Arrange these on the base of the pastry and put the flaked fish on top.

Beat the eggs and cream together and season well with black pepper and a pinch of nutmeg. It probably won't need salt. Pour into the pastry and bake for 5 minutes, then turn the oven temperature down to 300°F/150°C and cook for a further 35 minutes until golden on top and the pastry has shrunk slightly away from the sides of the pan.

Opposite: Forest mosses at Skellig Michael in County Kerry.

BAKED EGGS WITH SPINACH

SERVES 4 AS AN APPETIZER OR 2 AS A MAIN COURSE

½ lb/225 g spinach
1 tablespoon butter, plus extra for greasing
2 streaky bacon strips
salt and freshly ground black pepper
a few drops of soy sauce
4 large eggs, at room temperature
generous ½ cup/150 ml cream
chopped fresh chervil

Preheat the oven to 350°F/180°C. Wash the spinach and remove the stalks. Chop coarsely, place in a pan with a pat of butter, and simmer gently until just tender. Squeeze out the moisture. Broil the bacon until crisp and then chop finely.

Butter four individual ramekins. Put a tablespoon of spinach in each, sprinkle the bacon over the spinach, and season well, adding a drop or two of soy sauce to each ramekin. Crack the eggs into the ramekins and cover with the cream. Sprinkle the chervil over the top. Bake for 12–15 minutes until the egg whites are set and the yolks still soft.

Above: Michael's Stone Steps, Skellig, County Kerry.

SOUPS

SPRING GREEN SOUP

SERVES 6

Give yourself a spring boost with this green soup using the early shoots of nutrient rich herbs. You can vary the ingredients according to what can be foraged or found in your local grocery store or farmers' market.

large handful of sorrel leaves

large handful of spinach

handful of young nettles or dandelion greens

heart of a small green cabbage

4 tablespoons/55 g butter

2 onions, finely chopped

2 garlic cloves, chopped

chopped fresh thyme

2 potatoes, peeled and chopped

4¼ cups/1 liter chicken stock, or milk and water

generous ½ cup/150 ml cream

salt and freshly ground black pepper

Wash all the leaves thoroughly in salted water, removing any coarse stalks or ribs. Keep the nettles separate. Prepare the cabbage in the same way, shake dry, and finely chop.

Melt the butter in a large saucepan and gently sweat the onions, garlic, spinach, cabbage, sorrel, and thyme. Add the potatoes and the stock, or milk and water, and simmer until the potato is soft. Then add the nettles or dandelion greens and cook until they are tender, about 30 minutes.

Purée the soup, add the cream, adjust the seasoning, and serve.

Previous page: Evening at Lough Gill, County Sligo.

SPICY CARROT SOUP

1 tablespoon oil

1 tablespoon mustard seeds

2 tablespoons/30 g butter

2 medium onions, chopped

4–5 large carrots, grated

1 tablespoon coriander seeds

5 cups/1.2 liters chicken or vegetable stock

2 tablespoons rolled oats

3 teaspoons cider vinegar

juice and zest of 1 large orange

salt and freshly ground black pepper

heavy cream, to garnish (optional)

chopped cilantro, to garnish (optional)

Heat the oil in a large saucepan and add the mustard seeds, heating until they pop. Add the butter and onions and cook over low heat until they begin to soften. Then add the carrots and coriander seeds and continue cooking for 5–6 minutes. Add half the stock and the oats and cook a further few minutes.

If you like a smooth soup, purée the mixture at this point. Return it to the saucepan, add the vinegar, orange juice and zest, and the remaining stock. Season well with salt and pepper, simmer for a few moments, and serve.

The soup can be garnished with a swirl of cream and some chopped cilantro.

POTATO SOUP WITH SALMON AND CHIVES

SERVES 6

This rather unusual potato soup uses the excellent farm-raised salmon that is available all year round in Ireland.

6 oz/175 g piece of salmon, skin on

4 tablespoons/55 g butter

1 onion, finely chopped

2 leeks, chopped

6 medium potatoes, peeled and chopped

1 bay leaf

salt and freshly ground black pepper

2½ cups/600 ml chicken or fish stock

2½ cups/600 ml milk

2 tablespoons finely chopped fresh chives

Whole-Wheat Scones (see page 148) and butter, to serve

Put the salmon in a small saucepan, just barely cover with water, and poach gently until the fish is cooked, about 10 minutes. Remove from the water, skin, remove any bones, and flake. Use the water to make up the stock.

Melt the butter in a large saucepan and cook the onion and leeks until tender but not colored. Add the potatoes, bay leaf, salt and pepper, and the stock, and cook until the potatoes are soft. Remove the bay leaf, then purée in a food processor. Return to the saucepan. Next add the milk, chives, and salmon and heat through gently. Adjust the seasoning and serve hot. Whole-wheat scones with butter turn this soup into a little feast.

Opposite: Sunset over Lough Gill.

CRAB SOUP WITH SAFFRON

SERVES 6

4–5 saffron strands

6 large scallions, finely chopped

1 garlic clove

2 teaspoons fresh marjoram

2 tablespoons/30 g butter

scant 4 cups/900 ml fish or light chicken stock

1 tablespoon long-grain rice

1 tablespoon grated lemon zest

¾ lb/350 g cooked crab meat

generous ½ cup/150 ml cream

salt and freshly ground black pepper

1 tablespoon chopped fresh parsley, to garnish

Soak the saffron in a little water for 30 minutes. Cook the finely chopped scallions, garlic, and marjoram in the butter until soft. Add the stock, rice, lemon zest, and saffron, with its water, and simmer gently until the rice is soft. Add the crab and the cream and season well. Bring to a boil very gently, simmer for 2–3 minutes until hot, garnish with the parsley, and serve.

LOVAGE SOUP

SERVES 6

Lovage, once to be found in many Irish gardens, has celery-like leaves that make interesting soups and salads. Celery leaves are delicious prepared in the same way.

2 tablespoons/30 g butter
1 onion
1 garlic clove
2–3 large handfuls of young lovage leaves, chopped
1 tablespoon lemon juice, plus extra to taste
1 tablespoon all-purpose flour
2½ cups/600 ml hot chicken stock
2½ cups/600 ml milk
salt and freshly ground black pepper
4 tablespoons croûtons

Melt the butter in a large saucepan and cook the onion and garlic until soft. Add the chopped lovage and lemon juice. Cook until the leaves soften a little and then sprinkle in the flour. Continue stirring until the flour is cooked and the mixture is smooth. Gradually add half the hot stock, little by little, stirring well, until the soup has thickened and the leaves have cooked. Purée in a food processor or blender until smooth.

Return the soup to the saucepan, add the rest of the stock and the milk, and bring back to a boil. Season well with lemon juice, plenty of black pepper, and salt to taste. Just before serving sprinkle the croûtons over the top.

Note: To make croûtons, remove the crusts from 3 slices of white bread, cut into cubes, and fry in a little oil, until brown. Drain on paper towel.

PEA POD SOUP

SERVES 4

The pods of baby peas, so juicy and sweet, make very good soup with an intense pea taste. Sugar-snap peas give something of the same flavor.

½ lb/225 g sugar-snap peas
1 onion, finely chopped
2 tablespoons/30 g butter
1 oz/30 g all-purpose flour
3 cups/750 ml hot chicken or vegetable stock
fresh mint or summer savory, roughly chopped
½ teaspoon sugar
1 tablespoon chopped fresh parsley
salt and freshly ground black pepper
3–4 tablespoons cream
chopped fresh mint, to garnish

Wash the peas, put them in a large saucepan, and just cover with water. Simmer gently until the peas are just tender, about 15 minutes. Strain the peas and keep the water. In a large saucepan, cook the onion in the butter until soft. Mix in the flour and keep stirring until cooked, 2–3 minutes. Gradually add half the hot chicken or vegetable stock, stirring well until it thickens and the flour is cooked. Add the mint or savory. Add the peas and purée the mixture until smooth using a hand blender or food processor, then return it to the pan.

Add the remaining stock, the sugar, parsley, salt, and pepper. Check the seasoning and bring to a boil for 2–3 minutes. A little of the pea water can be added for a thinner soup. Serve in small bowls with a swirl of cream in each bowl. Garnish with mint.

WALNUT SOUP WITH WALNUT AND WATERCRESS SANDWICHES

SERVES 4

This simple soup is best made in the winter, when the new season's nuts are fresh. Good homemade stock will also greatly add to the flavor. This soup is traditionally popular with men—perhaps because it was frequently served in conjunction with game.

4 oz/110 g shelled walnuts

1 large garlic clove

scant 3 cups/675 ml chicken stock

1¼ cups/300 ml cream

salt and freshly ground black pepper

grated nutmeg

1 tablespoon finely chopped fresh chives or parsley, to garnish

FOR THE SANDWICHES

4 oz/110 g cream cheese

2 tablespoons finely chopped walnuts

2-3 tablespoons chopped watercress or flat-leaved parsley

6-8 thin slices of bread, preferably wheat or homemade

To make the soup, crush or blend the walnuts and garlic to a smooth paste, adding a little stock to help it along. Blend in the rest of the stock, add the cream, and season well, grating a very little nutmeg over it. Bring to a boil and simmer gently for 4-6 minutes before serving. Garnish with the herbs.

Make the sandwich spread by beating together the cream cheese, walnuts, and watercress. Remove the crusts from the bread, make the sandwiches, and cut them into quarters to serve.

CHESTNUT AND LENTIL SOUP

SERVES 6

With its warm color and earthy flavors, this lovely soup is redolent of autumn. Try a glass of not-too-dry sherry—an amontillado, perhaps, which is delicious with the soup; it's a fashion that is due for revival.

2 streaky bacon strips, finely chopped

2 large onions, finely chopped

2 garlic cloves, finely chopped

4 tablespoons/55 g butter

3 celery stalks with leaves, chopped

1 carrot, grated

generous 1 cup/225 g puréed chestnuts

1 cup/175 g green or brown lentils

1 teaspoon ground cumin

5 cups/1.2 liters chicken or vegetable stock

salt and freshly ground black pepper

generous ½ cup/150 ml cream, to serve

Put the bacon, onions, and garlic in a large saucepan with the butter and sauté until the bacon is crisp and the onions are soft. Add the chopped celery (reserve the leaves) and carrot and cook for 3-4 minutes. Stir in the chestnut purée. Add the lentils, cumin, and the stock and simmer gently until the lentils are soft.

Reserve one or two cups of the soup to give a little texture, and purée the rest. Return the purée to the reserved soup and check the seasoning. Reheat before dishing out the soup, swirl a spoonful of cream in each bowl, then scatter the chopped celery leaves over the top.

CELERY SOUP WITH BLUE CHEESE

SERVES 6

1 large head of celery

2 garlic cloves

1 onion

2 tablespoons/30 g butter

3 tablespoons/30 g all-purpose flour

5 cups/1.2 liters vegetable or light chicken stock

generous ½ cup/150 ml cream

salt and freshly ground black pepper

a little milk, if necessary

2–3 oz/55–75 g Chetwynde blue cheese
　　or other semi-hard blue cheese, crumbled

2–3 scallions, finely chopped, to garnish

crusty bread, to serve

Finely chop the celery, garlic, and onion. Melt the butter in a large saucepan, add the prepared vegetables, and stir frequently until they begin to soften. Sift in the flour and stir well until it has cooked. Gradually add the hot stock, mixing well to avoid lumps. Cook for 10 minutes or so until the vegetables are completely cooked, and then purée in a blender or food processor.

Return the soup to the saucepan, season well, and add the cream. (If the soup seems too thick, add a little milk also.) Cook for a few moments to amalgamate the cream.

Just before serving, bring back to a boil and stir in the crumbled cheese, but don't continue to boil once it has been added. Garnish with the finely chopped scallions. Serve with plenty of crusty bread.

MAINS

HAKE BAKED IN PAPER

SERVES 4

This method of cooking was widely used in the past to protect delicate morsels from the heat of the open fire. Writing paper was often specified in the recipes. Parchment paper, however is the ideal material, sealing in the flavors and appearing somehow more aesthetic on the plate than foil. Serve with a selection of roasted vegetables (see note).

4 hake fillets, weighing ¼ - ½ lb/110 - 225 g each
salt and freshly ground black pepper
4 tablespoons/55 g butter
1 large red pepper
1 teaspoon chopped fresh dill or marjoram
¼ cup/60 ml dry vermouth or white wine
8 - 10 live mussels, scrubbed and bearded, to garnish

Preheat the oven to 350°F/180°C.

Cut 4 pieces of parchment paper large enough to enclose the pieces of fish. Season and butter the fish well and place one on each piece of parchment. Slice the pepper into thin rounds, removing any seeds or white membrane, and place one or two slices on top of each piece of fish. Sprinkle a pinch of chopped dill or marjoram on each and pour on a tablespoon of vermouth or wine. Bring the two sides of the paper together and pleat lengthways, tucking the ends firmly under the package to seal.

Place the fish parcels in a baking dish and bake for about 20 - 25 minutes, depending on the thickness of the fillets. Steam the mussels open in a covered pan with a few tablespoons of water. Discard any that don't open. When the fish is ready, cut a slit in the paper with scissors, slide in the mussels and herbs, and serve.

Note: A mixture of seasonal vegetables, such as red and green peppers, celery, shallots, and zucchini, can be brushed with olive oil and roasted in the oven at the same time. Include some unpeeled garlic cloves and sprigs of thyme. Cut the vegetables into equal-size pieces and put them into the oven about 20 minutes before the fish goes in. They take about 40 minutes to cook in a hot oven.

Previous page: Slea Head and Coumeenoole Beach, County Kerry.

SALMON CAKES WITH DILL SAUCE

SERVES 4 AS A MAIN COURSE OR 8 AS AN APPETIZER

To make these fish cakes, use either a tail piece or cutlets or, better still, the buttery remains of a whole salmon.

1½ lb/675 g salmon

3 tablespoons finely chopped shallot

6 tablespoons/75 g butter, melted

1 egg yolk

1 tablespoon lemon juice

1 tablespoon finely chopped fresh herbs

salt and freshly ground black pepper

1¼ cups/140 g breadcrumbs

1 tablespoon cream, if necessary

1 egg, beaten

2 tablespoons each whole-wheat flour and breadcrumbs, mixed

oil, for frying

fresh green salad, to serve

FOR THE DILL SAUCE

1 tablespoon butter

1 tablespoon all-purpose flour

1 cup/240 ml hot milk

3–4 tablespoons crème fraîche

2 tablespoons finely chopped fresh dill or 2 teaspoons dried dill

salt and freshly ground black pepper

Poach the salmon in lightly salted water for 12–15 minutes. Remove any skin and bones and flake the fish. Sauté the shallot in a little of the butter until soft.

Mix together the salmon, shallot, egg yolk, lemon juice, all but 1 tablespoon of the melted butter, the herbs, salt, and pepper. Add the ¼ cup/140 g of breadcrumbs and work well together. Add a spoonful of cream if the mixture is too dry. Flour your hands well, then shape into 4 or 8 cakes, patting them firmly into shape. Dip each one into the beaten egg and then into the breadcrumb and flour mixture to coat.

Heat the remaining butter and oil in a large frying pan and cook the cakes for 5–6 minutes on each side until crisp and very hot.

Meanwhile, to make the sauce, melt the butter in a saucepan, whisk in the flour, and stir until cooked, about a minute. Off the heat, gradually whisk in the hot milk. Bring back to a boil and stir until the sauce thickens. Remove from the heat, add the crème fraîche and dill, and season to taste.

Drain the salmon cakes on paper towel and serve with the dill sauce and a green salad.

LIMA BEAN HOT POT

SERVES 4–5

This is the kind of homey, comforting supper we all love to come home to.

½ lb/225 g dried lima beans, soaked overnight
¾ lb/350 g cubed bacon
oil, for frying
1 lb/450 g onions, sliced
1 lb/450 tart cooking apples, peeled and sliced
1 lb/450 g potatoes, sliced
salt and freshly ground black pepper
chopped fresh thyme
1 or 2 fresh sage leaves
1¼ cups/300 ml stock or water

Drain the beans, cover with fresh water, bring to a boil, and boil for 10 minutes, then simmer gently until almost soft but not breaking up, about 40 minutes.

Preheat the oven to 300°F/150°C. In a heavy pan, brown the meat in a little oil. Remove the meat, then brown the onions in the same pan. Layer the onions, bacon, apples, potatoes, and beans in a greased ovenproof casserole dish, sprinkle with pepper and thyme, and tuck in the sage leaves. Finish with a layer of potatoes. Add a very little salt, lots of black pepper, and pour the stock over all. Cover with foil or a lid, and bake for about 1½ hours.

Remove the foil and continue cooking until the potatoes are brown. Add a little more stock, if necessary. A simple green salad is all you need with this.

Above: Slea Head ruins, County Kerry.

FRICASSÉE OF PORK

SERVES 6

1 large onion, chopped

2 tablespoons/30 g butter

1 tablespoon oil

¾ lb/350 g button mushrooms

2 lb/900 g boneless pork, cubed

1 tablespoon all-purpose flour

2 teaspoons ground cumin

generous ½ cup/150 ml dry white wine or stock

1¼ cups/300 ml cream

salt and freshly ground black pepper

2 celery stalks, thinly sliced

Below: Portmagee Village, County Kerry.

Preheat the oven to 300°F/150°C. In a pan, soften the onion in half the butter and oil, then transfer to an ovenproof dish. Add the mushrooms to the pan and cook for a few minutes until lightly browned. Pour, with any juice, into the dish. Toss the cubed pork in the flour and cumin and brown in the pan with the remaining oil and butter. Add to the dish. Sprinkle any remaining flour into the pan and stir for a few moments to cook. Add the wine or stock, scraping up all the sediment thoroughly. Now add the cream, check and adjust the seasoning, and stir well.

Pour over the pork mixture, stir in the thinly sliced celery, cover, and cook gently until the pork is tender, 45-60 minutes. Serve with creamy mashed potatoes, rice, or noodles.

CHICKEN AND CHEESE WRAPPED IN BACON

SERVES 4

Cashel Blue cheese from Tipperary (available in cheese shops) gives just the right note of acidity to the chicken. You will need cocktail sticks or cooking thread to secure the rolls.

4 boneless, skinless chicken breasts
8 strips of streaky bacon
2–3 fresh sage leaves, torn
salt and freshly ground black pepper
lemon zest
6 oz/175 g Cashel Blue cheese (or other blue cheese)
2 tablespoons/30 g butter
½ cup/125 ml white wine, vermouth, or chicken stock
2–3 tablespoons cream
crisp green salad or fresh vegetables, to serve

TO GARNISH
lemon wedges
fresh sage leaves

Place a chicken breast flat on a chopping board and, with a sharp knife, slice it in two horizontally. Repeat with the others and cover each piece with plastic wrap and beat gently with a rolling pin until slightly larger. Cut each bacon strip in two and stretch them out by stroking with the blade of a large knife. Lay two pieces of bacon side by side on the board, put a small piece of sage on top and cover with a piece of chicken. Season the chicken well and add some lemon zest.

Cut the cheese into 8 fingers and place one on each piece of chicken, roll up the bacon and chicken, and secure with cocktail sticks or thread. Continue with the rest of the bacon and chicken until you have 8 rolls. In a heavy pan, brown the rolls in the butter, turning frequently, for about 10 minutes until the chicken is cooked and the cheese is beginning to melt.

Transfer the rolls to a hot dish and remove the cocktail sticks or thread. Add the wine, vermouth, or stock to the pan, scraping up all the sediment, and bubbling well for a few moments to reduce the wine. Add the cream, bubble again for 2–3 minutes, then check and adjust the seasoning. Pour a little sauce onto the center of each plate and arrange the rolls on top.

Garnish with lemon wedges and a few sage leaves. Serve with a crisp salad or a green vegetable.

Opposite: Ogham Stones, Kilmalkader, County Kerry.

SPRING LAMB CUTLETS IN PASTRY

SERVES 4

Easter is the time of renewal, and lamb symbolizes the return of life in many cultures. Roast baby lamb is the traditional Easter Sunday dinner and is pure magic, especially when it's moist and tender and delicately pink. As a change from the usual leg of lamb, try this rack of lamb in pastry, a great party dish and very easy to carve—simply cut down between the bones. You will need 2 cutlets per person, possibly 3 if they are very tiny. This sauce is the invariable sauce for lamb in Ireland and it's very much an eighteenth-century idea, the vinegar counteracting the fattiness of the meat.

1 frenched rack of lamb (about 8 ribs)
4 tablespoons/55 g butter
salt and freshly ground black pepper
4 shallots, finely chopped
½ lb/225 g mushrooms, finely chopped
4 oz/110 g dried apricots, finely chopped
chopped fresh mint or oregano
grated lemon zest and juice
1 lb/450 g puff pastry
1 egg, beaten, to glaze

FOR THE MINT SAUCE
1–2 tablespoons chopped fresh mint, or to taste
1–2 tablespoons sugar or apple butter, or to taste
1–2 tablespoons hard cider or white wine vinegar
3–4 tablespoons water

Preheat the oven to 425°F/220°C. Rub the lamb with half the butter and season well. Roast the meat for 8–10 minutes, depending on the size of the ribs. Allow to cool completely.

Gently cook the shallots, mushrooms, apricots, and mint or oregano in the remaining butter until the juices have thickened. Season this well with lemon zest and a little lemon juice and plenty of black pepper. Press the stuffing between the ribs. Roll out the pastry into a sheet large enough to enclose the rack and fold around the meat, allowing the bones to stick out through the pastry. Cover these with foil to prevent them from burning.

Decorate with pastry trimmings, if desired. Brush over the pastry with the beaten egg. Heat the oven to 350°F/180°C and bake until the pastry is browned, about 25–30 minutes.

Meanwhile, to make the sauce, bring all the ingredients to a boil, then remove from the heat, stirring to dissolve the sugar. Allow to cool. Serve the lamb with mint sauce.

IRISH STEW

SERVES 6

There is much argument concerning the authentic Irish stew, but for most of us, I suspect, the "authentic" dish is the one made in our own families. The pure tradition uses only mutton, potatoes, onion, thyme, salt, and pepper, and this, I think, is generally agreed to be the thing. In my home, barley was included and some contemporary recipes include carrots, and even celery, so you can make your own choice.

1 lb/450 g onions
2½ lb/1.15 kg potatoes
2 lb/900 g neck of lamb chops
salt and white pepper
2 tablespoons/30 g butter
2 carrots, chopped
2 celery stalks, chopped
1 large fresh thyme sprig
2 cups/450 ml water or lamb stock

Chop the onions coarsely. Peel and thickly slice the potatoes. Season the chops well with salt and pepper.

Put the butter in the bottom of a heavy saucepan and then layer in the meat and vegetables, finishing with a layer of potatoes. Bury the thyme in the center. Pour in the stock or water. Cover the pan tightly with foil and a lid, bring to a boil, and then immediately lower the heat and cook gently on the lowest possible heat for about 1½ hours. The meat and vegetables should cook in their juices with very little liquid left at the end, so watch for burning. It may be necessary to add more liquid.

Note: The stew can also be cooked in the oven. If barley is included it's less likely to burn in the oven.

CORNED BEEF AND CABBAGE

SERVES 6–8

"Corned" beef, an old word for pickled beef, can be prepared at home using the same method as for Spiced Beef (page 84), only leaving out the spices. This process takes 10 days, or you can use ready-pickled beef.

3–4 lb/1.3–1.8 kg beef brisket

FOR THE BRINE
¾ cup/225 g salt
1 teaspoon saltpeter (optional)
½ cup/115 g brown sugar
1¼ cups/300 ml Guinness
6½ cups/1.5 liters cold water

FOR THE DISH
1 tablespoon brown sugar
1 tablespoon mustard powder
2–3 cloves
2 carrots, sliced
2 celery stalks, sliced
1 onion, sliced
1 green or savoy cabbage
Dijon mustard and boiled potatoes with butter, to serve

In a good sized saucepan, combine the salt, saltpeter, brown sugar, and Guinness. Pour in the cold water, then bring slowly to a boil, turn down the heat, and simmer for 10 minutes. Turn off the heat and allow to cool fully. In a large non-reactive container (such as plastic, ceramic, glass, or stainless steel), cover the meat with the cooled brine (making sure it is completely submerged) and transfer to the fridge for 10 days, turning the meat in the brine every day. Then drain the meat, discarding the liquid, and pat dry. (If you are using ready-pickled beef, soak the meat for several hours in cold water.)

When ready to cook the dish, combine the meat with the sugar, spices, carrots, celery, and onion in a large saucepan. Cover with cold water and bring it to a boil very slowly. Simmer gently for about 1–1½ hours (20 minutes per 1 lb/450 g). When the meat is tender, turn off the heat and let it rest it in the water for 30 minutes while you prepare the cabbage.

Wash and quarter the cabbage and put it in a large saucepan with a ladleful of the cooking water from the meat. Pour in enough boiling water to cover half the depth of the cabbage. Boil hard, without a lid, until the cabbage is just tender. Drain and keep warm while you slice the beef. Arrange the meat on a deep dish and put the cabbage around it.

Serve with mustard and plain boiled potatoes, and of course, plenty of butter for the spuds (potatoes).

Note: The traditional method is to put the cabbage into the pot with the meat for the last 15 minutes of cooking time, but I feel the rather lean meat benefits from a resting period and the cabbage is less greasy when cooked on its own.

Saltpeter is not essential, rather it is used to preserve the color of the meat. it is available online or you can use Prague Powder number 1 (also known as curing salt), which can be purchased from a meat-curing butcher or specialty store.

CHICKEN AND HAM PASTIES

MAKES 4

These traditional pasties are ideal "make-ahead" food for summer eating. Pair them with salad and chutney, or baby potatoes for lunches and family dinners, or pack them in boxes for days at the beach.

2 small leeks, finely chopped

3½ oz/100 g mushrooms, sliced

4 tablespoons/55 g butter

1 tablespoon all-purpose flour

1¼ cups/300 ml hot milk

salt and freshly ground black pepper

¼ teaspoon coriander seeds

½ lb/225 g cooked chicken, finely chopped

½ lb/225 g cooked ham, finely chopped

1 teaspoon poppyseeds

FOR THE PASTRY

2 sticks/225 g butter, cubed

scant 3 cups/400 g all-purpose flour

salt, to taste

2–4 tablespoons cold water

1 small egg, beaten, to glaze

Preheat the oven to 375°F/190°C and grease a baking sheet.

Make the pastry in the usual way, by rubbing the butter into the flour and salt and moistening it with 2–4 tablespoons of cold water, then roll it out and cut into four 6 inch/15 cm circles. Chill while you make the filling.

Sauté the leeks with the mushrooms in 2 tablespoons/30 g butter. Set aside. Melt the remaining butter in a saucepan, stir in the flour, and cook for 2–3 minutes. Gradually add the hot milk, stirring continuously, until the sauce thickens smoothly. Season well. Add the coriander seeds and the leek mixture and its juices. Cool completely.

Fold the finely chopped meats into the sauce and divide among the pastry circles. Dampen the edges with a little of the beaten egg, then draw up the 2 sides together, pinching well to seal. Place, seam-side down, on the greased baking sheet. Brush with the remaining beaten egg and sprinkle with poppyseeds. Bake until the pastry is golden, 20–25 minutes.

MACKEREL WITH GOOSEBERRY SAUCE

SERVES 6

This is a combination that has its origins in the past, when fruit sauces with fish or meat were considered good for the digestion. Apple sauce with pork is another example. The elderflowers give a delicate muscatel flavor and were often added to apple and gooseberry tarts. Pick the elderflowers well away from dusty roadsides. The sauce can be either hot or cold and it's equally good with kippers or pork. This dish is great with baby potatoes, perked up with finely chopped scallions and lots of black pepper.

6 mackerel, scaled and cleaned
salt and freshly ground black pepper
2 tablespoons all-purpose flour
1 egg, beaten
3 tablespoons fine oatmeal
butter and oil, for frying
boiled baby potatoes and finely chopped scallions, to serve

FOR THE GOOSEBERRY SAUCE
1 lb/450 g gooseberries
1–2 elderflower heads
sugar, to taste

To make the sauce, gently cook the gooseberries and elderflowers with 2–3 tablespoons of water until soft. Remove the elderflowers, sweeten to taste, and push through a sieve. Set aside.

Clean and dry the mackerel, removing the heads if preferred. Season the insides and flour well. Dip the mackerel in the beaten egg, then roll in the oatmeal. Melt a tablespoon each of butter and oil in a large non-stick frying pan and fry the mackerel over low heat until the flesh is opaque. Drain on paper towel and serve with the gooseberry sauce.

BAKED SALMON ENCRUSTED WITH HERBS

SERVES 6–7

For maximum effect and not too much effort, this baked salmon has it all. Ask your fishmonger to split your fish lengthways into two long fillets. A 3 lb/1.3 kg fish will be enough for 6 with side dishes.

1 inch/2.5 cm cube of fresh ginger

6 canned anchovies, drained

1 stick/110 g butter

3 tablespoons finely chopped fresh parsley

3 tablespoons finely chopped scallions

grated zest of 1 lemon

3–5 lb/1.3 kg–2.25 kg salmon, filleted

about ¾ cup/75 g breadcrumbs, made from day-old bread

salt and freshly ground black pepper

FOR THE SAUCE

3 egg yolks

1¼ cups/300 ml cream

5–6 sorrel leaves, ribs removed, leaves chopped

grated zest of 1 lemon

1 tablespoon fresh chopped cilantro or parsley

Preheat the oven to 325°F/160°C.

Mash the ginger to a paste with the anchovies, 5 tablespoons/75 g of the butter, the parsley, scallions, and grated zest of half the lemon. Butter a sheet of parchment paper that will fit the salmon and use it to line a large baking sheet. Lay one salmon fillet on the paper, skin-side down, and spread with half the herb butter. Lay the other fillet on top, skin-side up, reversing the wide end over the narrow end of the bottom fillet. Spread the remaining herb butter on top. Cover the salmon with the breadcrumbs, patting them down lightly, season well, and dot with the remaining butter.

Bake for 12 minutes per 1 lb/450 g for smaller fish, but a 6–7 lb/2.7–3.2 kg fish will not require more than an hour.

Meanwhile, make the sauce. Season the egg yolks and beat them together. Bring the cream to a boil with the sorrel leaves and lemon zest and cook to reduce for a few moments. Cool slightly, then pour slowly into the yolks, stirring all the time. Return to the saucepan and over a low heat, cook, stirring continuously without allowing it to boil, until the sauce thickens slightly.

When the fish is cooked, use the parchment paper to lift the fish on to a heated serving dish and strain the buttery fish juices into the sauce. Add the cilantro or parsley and serve.

Note: if the sauce shows signs of becoming lumpy, scrape immediately into a blender and purée for a few seconds.

SCALLOPS WITH TARRAGON SAUCE

SERVES OR 3–4 AS A MAIN COURSE OR 6 AS AN APPETIZER, DEPENDING ON THE SIZE OF THE SCALLOPS

Tender, juicy scallops need very little cooking. Be sure to save the red corals when cleaning them.

¾ cup/175 ml white wine

scant ½ cup/100 ml water

grated zest and juice of ½ lemon

4–5 fresh tarragon leaves or a pinch of dried tarragon

12 scallops, cleaned

scant ½ cup/100 ml cream

1 tablespoon butter

3 egg yolks, beaten

1 tablespoon finely chopped fresh parsley

mixed baby salad greens, to garnish

2 teaspoons paprika

Put the wine, water, lemon juice and zest, and tarragon leaves together in a saucepan and boil for 2–3 minutes. Add the scallops and corals and gently poach for 3–5 minutes, depending on size, until they are no longer translucent and just firm to the touch. Remove to a warm place.

Strain the cooking liquid into a small saucepan and boil rapidly to reduce slightly. Add the cream and butter and simmer for 5–6 minutes. Now pour slowly into the egg yolks, whisking well as you pour. Return the mixture to the saucepan over very low heat and continue to stir until the sauce thickens slightly, being careful not to let it boil. Season well with salt and pepper and add the parsley and more tarragon to taste.

Arrange the scallops on warm plates and pour the sauce over them. Add a little pile of dressed salad leaves to each plate and finish with a dusting of paprika.

Below: Slea Head and Blasket Islands, Dingle Peninsula, County Kerry.

HAM IN PASTRY

SERVES 10 AS A MAIN COURSE OR 25 AS PART OF A PARTY SUPPER

Hams, and the art of cooking them, are well understood in Ireland and they are always popular for grand occasions. If the ham is to be eaten hot, seasonal vegetables and a well-made parsley sauce are the traditional partners. Rowan berry jelly or redcurrant jelly heated with a glass of port and a little orange juice also makes an excellent sauce.

6-8 lb/2.8-3.6 kg uncooked cured ham (or use an uncut cooked
    ham and skip the cooking steps)
juniper berries
2 bay leaves
1 large onion, halved
2-3 tablespoons brown sugar
1 tablespoon mustard powder
2 lb/900 g puff or shortcrust pastry
2 tablespoons Dijon-type mild mustard
1 egg, beaten, to glaze

Soak the ham overnight in cold water if it seems to be salty; otherwise 1-2 hours will do.

When ready to cook, put the ham in a large saucepan with a few juniper berries, the bay leaves, and the onion halves. Add the sugar and mustard powder, cover with cold water, then bring to a boil slowly and, timing from when the water boils, simmer for 20 minutes per 1 lb/450 g. Test before the last 20 minutes, as it may not be necessary because the ham will cook a little more in the oven. (Skip the above steps if using cooked ham.)

When cooked, allow to cool for about 30 minutes in the water, then remove and peel off the skin and some of the fat if there is too much. Allow the ham to cool further.

Preheat the oven to 375°F/190°C. Roll out the pastry into a large square that will cover the ham, keeping it a little thicker than usual. Rub Dijon mustard over the ham and then drape the pastry over the ham; cover it completely, tucking the pastry underneath, trimming the surplus, and dampening and sealing the joins. Place on a baking sheet, keeping the seams underneath as much as possible. Brush with the beaten egg. Use the trimmings to make decorative leaves etc. and brush these with the egg again. Make a vent at the highest point.

Bake for about 20 minutes. If serving the ham hot, cover the pastry loosely with foil and lower the heat to 325°F/160°C for another 45 minutes or so to ensure the ham is completely heated through.

JELLIED TONGUE

SERVES 6 AS A MAIN COURSE OR 8–10 AS PART OF A PARTY SUPPER

Liked and disliked with equal intensity, a pressed pickled tongue is an essential ingredient of any Irish cold meat platter and, though it takes a long time to cook, the preparation is extremely simple. A little port added to the stock gives a zing to the jelly. Small, ready-trimmed tongues are widely available and usually don't need to be soaked; larger tongues may need soaking overnight.

1 beef tongue, weighing about 2 lb/900 g

1 each onion, carrot, and celery stick

1 or 2 cloves or ½ star anise

2 teaspoons black peppercorns

1 orange

4 teaspoons/11 g or ½ oz sachet/3 leaves unflavored gelatine

a glass of port

spicy Cumberland sauce or horseradish sauce, to serve

Place the tongue in a large saucepan and cover with cold water. Add the vegetables, cloves, peppercorns, and a large strip of orange zest. Bring to a boil very slowly and simmer gently until a skewer will slide in easily. This can take from 2–4 hours, depending on its size. Remove the tongue from the water and, when cool enough to handle, peel off the skin and any gristle. Return the tongue to the stock, to keep warm.

Strain 1 ¼ cups/300 ml of the cooking liquid and use a little to dissolve the gelatine, according to the package directions. Put the remainder in a small saucepan with the port and the juice of ½ the orange. Boil hard to reduce for 1–2 minutes; cool slightly, then add the dissolved gelatine. Put the warm tongue in a bowl or mold that will just hold it. Pour over enough of the port jelly to cover it when it is pressed down well with a plate or saucer. Put a weight on top of the plate (tin cans or a stone) and leave overnight. Set aside any remaining port jelly to set, for the garnish.

To serve, remove any fat from the top, turn out the tongue, and carve in thin slices. Decorate with the chopped jelly. Spicy Cumberland sauce or horseradish cream sauce can be served with it.

RAGOUT OF SCALLOPS AND BACON

SERVES 4

8 large scallops, cleaned

2 tablespoons/30 g butter

4 streaky bacon strips

1 onion, chopped

2–3 scallions, chopped

½ lb/225 g mixed shiitake and oyster mushrooms

2 teaspoons all-purpose flour

generous ½ cup/150 ml white wine

generous ½ cup/150 ml cream

1 tablespoon chopped fresh parsley

1 teaspoon chopped fresh dill or chervil

1 tablespoon lemon juice

salt and freshly ground black pepper

creamy, buttery mashed potatoes, to serve

Carefully remove the red corals, then neatly slice the scallops into 3 pieces horizontally.

Melt 1 tablespoon/15 g of the butter in a medium pan and gently sauté the scallops with the corals for 1 minute, then set aside. In the same pan, fry the bacon until crisp, then remove and chop finely. Cook the onions, scallions, and mushrooms in the fat from the bacon, adding the remaining butter, for 2–3 minutes, then sprinkle in the flour, stirring well until the flour is cooked. Stir in the wine and bubble gently, stirring until the sauce thickens, then add the cream, bacon, parsley, dill, and a little lemon juice. Check the seasoning and bring back to a boil. Return the scallops and allow to heat through, 1–2 minutes.

Creamy, buttery mashed potatoes are the perfect partner for this rich ragout.

Opposite: Dun Aengus stone fort, Aran Islands, County Galway.
Overleaf: Skellig Michael, Iveragh Peninsula, County Kerry.

BRAISED STUFFED PHEASANTS
WITH IRISH WHISKEY SAUCE

SERVES 4–6 (LARGE COCK PHEASANTS WILL SERVE 3 PEOPLE GENEROUSLY, BUT HENS ARE CONSIDERED FINER EATING)

Pheasants are in plentiful supply from October to January and are usually sold prepared and neatly packed at the butcher or supermarket. Braising the birds keeps them moist and tender.

2 pheasants

6 tablespoons/75 g butter

6 celery stalks, roughly chopped

4 carrots, roughly chopped

4 onions, roughly chopped

fresh parsley and thyme sprigs

1¼ cups/300 ml chicken stock

salt and freshly ground black pepper

4 tablespoons redcurrant jelly

1 cup/250 ml Irish whiskey

1¼ cups/300 ml cream

FOR THE STUFFING

¼ lb/110 g hazelnuts

4 tablespoons/55 g butter

1 tablespoon each finely chopped carrot, celery, and onion

2 streaky bacon strips, chopped

zest of 1 orange, plus 1 tablespoon juice

6 tablespoons cooked wild and basmati rice mixture

1 tablespoon Irish whiskey

chestnuts and game chips, to garnish (optional, see note)

To make the stuffing, lightly brown the hazelnuts in a heavy pan, rub off any loose skins, and finely chop the nuts. In the same pan, melt a pat of butter and sauté the chopped vegetables and bacon. Add the orange zest, rice, and the remaining butter. Moisten with a tablespoon each of whiskey and orange juice. Season well. When cold, stuff the birds loosely and secure with a cocktail stick. Wrap any surplus stuffing in foil and put in the pot with the birds.

In a heavy casserole dish that will just fit the two birds, melt 4 tablespoons/55 g of the butter and brown the birds all over. Remove. Put in the chopped vegetables and a few sprigs of parsley and thyme. Lay the birds on top, on their sides, and pour in the stock. Season the birds well. Cover the casserole dish, sealing it well with foil, if necessary. Cook gently for 20 minutes. Then turn the pheasants and cook for a further 15–20 minutes. Test by inserting a skewer between the leg and the breast. The liquid should be faintly pink; pheasants do not benefit from overcooking. Remove the birds and keep them warm.

Strain off the liquid from the vegetables and remove as much fat as possible. Blend the liquid with the redcurrant jelly and pour into a small saucepan. Add the whiskey, heat for a few moments, and then ignite to burn off the alcohol and concentrate the flavor. Now add the cream, taste for seasoning, and boil hard to reduce. Finally, whisk in a little butter. Arrange the birds on a large serving dish, tuck the feathers under the tails (if you have them), and glaze with a little of the sauce. Pheasants are traditionally garnished with chestnuts and game chips, or served on a bed of spinach dressed in butter and garlic.

Note: To prepare chestnuts, make a cross in the skins with a sharp knife and simmer for 20 minutes; cool and peel. Return to the water and continue cooking until they are tender. Cooked chestnuts can be bought vac-packed or canned. Game chips are homemade potato chips, made by slicing peeled potatoes very thinly into cold water. Remove from the water, dry, and fry in hot oil. Drain and sprinkle with salt.

LAMB WITH CRAB-APPLE JELLY

SERVES 4–6

Crab apples can often be found for the taking, in woodland areas and along roadsides. They are abundant in Killarney, and their wild and winey flavor gives character to this simple sauce. Ordinary apple jelly can be enhanced by the addition of a little redcurrant jelly or use Rowan Berry Jelly (see page 170).

1–2 racks of lamb (4–6 cutlets each)

sea salt and freshly ground black pepper

3 tablespoons olive oil

1 cup/250 ml each of red wine and stock

3 large garlic cloves

2–3 fresh rosemary sprigs or 1 teaspoon dried rosemary

2 tablespoons dried pink peppercorns (rose peppers; if you can only find the brined ones, rise off the brine and use only 1 tablespoon)

3 tablespoons crab-apple jelly

lemon juice, to taste

2 tablespoons/30 g butter, chilled and cubed

fresh rosemary sprigs, to garnish

Trim the lamb of any excess fat and neatly french the rack. Season with black pepper and rub over with some of the olive oil. Place in a deep dish and pour the wine and stock over the meat. Crush the garlic cloves and tuck them, with the rosemary, around the meat. Marinate for at least half an hour, or overnight.

When ready to cook, preheat the oven to 425°F/220°C.

Remove the meat from the marinade and blot dry with paper towel. In a hot pan, brown the racks briefly in a spoonful of oil. Rub a little more oil over the meat and sprinkle the skin with salt. Roast for 15–16 minutes for pink lamb, and 5 minutes or so longer if you prefer it less pink. Transfer the lamb to a dish, cover it with foil and a dish towel, and allow it to rest.

Strain the marinade into a saucepan and add a sprig of rosemary and the pink peppercorns. Boil rapidly to reduce, then add the crab-apple jelly, whisking well to dissolve. Taste, adding a little lemon juice if it's too sweet. Pour any juices from the roasting pan into the sauce, remove the rosemary, and whisk in the butter, a piece at a time.

Slice the lamb into cutlets, 2 or 3 per person, depending on size. Pour a small pool of sauce on each plate and arrange the cutlets on top. Garnish with the rosemary sprigs.

ROAST MICHAELMAS GOOSE WITH PRUNE, APPLE, AND POTATO STUFFING

SERVES 6

The tradition of a goose for dinner on the feast of St Michael (September 29) is as old as that of the Christmas goose, and made good sense: geese born in the spring were turned out to fatten among the stubble after the grain was harvested, making them nice and plump for Michaelmas.

10-12 lb/4-5.5 kg goose

1 onion, sliced

1 tablespoon/25 g butter

¾ lb/350 g prunes, soaked, pitted, and chopped

1 lb/450 g apples, chopped

1 lb/450 g potatoes, cooked and mashed

1 teaspoon caraway seeds

1 tablespoon Dijon mustard

1 tablespoon orange zest

1 tablespoon chopped fresh sage or ½ teaspoon dried

1 tablespoon sea salt

freshly ground black pepper

gravy (see note) and Sautéed Cabbage with Bacon (see page 106), to serve

To drain some of the fat and dry the skin in readiness for roasting crisply, prick the goose thoroughly all over with a fork. Pour boiling water over the skin and leave to dry in an airy place while you make the stuffing.

Preheat the oven to 425°F/220°C.

Cook the sliced onion in the butter until soft, then mix with the chopped prunes, apples, and mashed potatoes. Add the caraway seeds, mustard, orange zest, and herbs and season well. When ready to cook, pack the stuffing loosely into the cavity and put any surplus into a foil-covered dish to cook separately. Secure the legs in place by passing a skewer through the first joint of one leg through to the other leg, or tie securely in place.

Dry the goose skin with paper towel and rub well with the sea salt. Sit the goose, breast-side down, on a rack in a deep roasting pan and cook for 40 minutes, turning the goose breast-side up after 20 minutes. Lower the heat to 300°F/150°C. Allow about 20 minutes for each 1 lb/450 g and test by inserting a skewer between the leg and the breast; clear liquid indicates that it is done. There will be a great deal of fat, so it is more manageable to pour it off once or twice during cooking (you can reserve the fat for roasting potatoes). When the goose is ready, cover it with foil and a dish towel and set aside to rest for at least 30-40 minutes.

Serve with gravy and sautéed cabbage.

Note: To make a gravy, add a little stock (preferably made from the giblets, etc. and ½ cup/125 ml of wine or 2 tablespoons orange juice) to the de-fatted sediment in the roasting pan, scraping it up well. Boil to reduce, then whisk in a few knobs of butter or a little cream.

Opposite: Killarney Lake, County Kerry.

PORK AND APPLE PIE

SERVES 4 AS A MAIN COURSE OR 8 AS AN APPETIZER

This pie is based on a recipe by Hannah Glasse from her famous 1758 cookbook, The Art of Cookery Made Plain and Easy. *This book circulated so widely in Ireland it was said that in some homes of the day it was the only book!*

2 large onions, peeled and finely chopped

2 tablespoons/30 g butter (or more if using pork meat)

2 lb/900 g good sausage meat or equal quantities of pork pieces and pork belly, finely ground

¼ lb/110 g streaky bacon, finely chopped

1½ lb/675 g eating or cooking apples, chopped

2 tablespoons/30 g brown sugar

salt, freshly ground black pepper, and grated nutmeg

2–3 fresh sage leaves, chopped, or a little dried sage

5–6 juniper berries, lightly crushed

½ cup/125 ml white wine or hard cider

1 egg, beaten, to glaze

FOR THE PASTRY

2 sticks/225 g butter

1 lb/450 g all-purpose flour

pinch of salt

1 egg

1–2 tablespoons very cold water

Make the pastry in the usual way, by rubbing the butter into the flour, adding a pinch of salt, and moistening the mixture with the egg and water, and leave the dough to rest. Line a greased 9 inch/23 cm square cake pan with parchment paper. Roll out two-thirds of the pastry until it is large enough to line the pan. Roll out the remainder for the lid. Keep any trimmings to make decorations.

Preheat the oven to 350°F/180°C.

Sauté the onions in half the butter until soft. Cool and add to the sausage meat, bacon, apples, and sugar. Season well with pepper, a little salt, and a good grating of nutmeg. Put in the sage (be sparing if using dried). Spread the meat in the pastry base, pushing the juniper berries down into the mixture. Pour in the wine or cider and dot with the remaining butter. If using pork pieces, add more butter (about 2 tablespoons/25 g more). Cover with the pastry lid, dampening and pressing the edges together well. Make leaves with the pastry trimmings to decorate the pie and then brush the top with the beaten egg.

Bake for about 1 hour, covering the top with foil if it starts to get too brown. When cold, cut into squares and serve with a green salad, fruity chutney, and good bread.

Note: this pie improves in flavor if it can be left in the fridge for a day or two before cutting.

CHICKEN PIE WITH CASHEWS

SERVES 4–6

This chicken pie is ideal comfort food for cold evenings.
The cashews can be replaced by toasted whole almonds.

1 onion, chopped

3 carrots

1 bay leaf

2 celery stalks

4 large chicken breasts

2 chicken legs

1 tablespoon oil

3 oz/75 g cashews

8 shallots, peeled

chopped fresh or dried tarragon

2 tablespoons all-purpose flour

2 tablespoons butter

salt, freshly ground black pepper, and grated nutmeg

FOR THE TOPPING

1½ lb/675 g potatoes

2 tablespoons/30 g butter

hot milk

In a large pot, combine the onion, 1 carrot, the bay leaf, and 4 cups/900 ml water, bring to a boil, lower the heat, and simmer for 40 minutes to make a stock. Remove the carrot and bay leaf from the stock. Cut the remaining carrots and the celery into thick slices and add, with the chicken, to the stock. Cook until the vegetables are just tender but not soft, then remove with a slotted spoon. Remove the breasts as soon as they are just cooked, after 12–15 minutes, and continue cooking the legs until they are tender.

Skin and bone the chicken legs and put the meat with the breasts. Cut the meat into neat pieces. Return the trimmings to the stock and boil hard to reduce until you have about 2½ cups/600 ml. Strain the stock and set aside. Preheat the oven to 400°F/200°C.

In a small pan, heat a teaspoon of oil and toast the nuts for a few moments; remove the nuts and cook the shallots in the same pan until they are nicely browned. Add a small ladleful of stock and continue to cook until they are tender. Arrange the nuts, vegetables, and the chicken pieces in a pie or casserole dish and season well. Add a little chopped fresh tarragon (less if using dried).

In a large saucepan, cook the flour in the melted butter and then gradually add the remaining hot stock, stirring well until the sauce thickens. Season well with salt, pepper, and nutmeg and pour over the chicken and vegetables in the pie dish.

Boil the potatoes in their skins until tender, then drain, peel, and mash vigorously. Add the butter, fluff with a fork, and add just enough hot milk to make them creamy. Spread the mashed potatoes over the chicken and cook on the top shelf of the oven until the sauce is bubbling and the potatoes are golden brown.

BAKED COD WITH MUSHROOMS

SERVES 4–6

1 medium onion

1 leek, cleaned

4 tablespoons/55 g butter

salt and freshly ground black pepper

4–6 cod cutlets or fillets

½ lb/240 g mushrooms, sliced

grated zest of ½ lemon

2 tablespoons all-purpose flour

1¼ cups/300 ml hot fish stock or milk

6 anchovy fillets, split in half (optional)

¼ cup/30 g breadcrumbs

chopped fresh parsley, to garnish

Preheat the oven to 325°F/170°C.

Chop the onion finely and slice the leek. Cook them gently in half the butter until soft. Spread them in a buttered ovenproof dish. Season the fish and place it on top.

In the same pan, melt the remaining butter and cook the sliced mushrooms and lemon zest for several minutes until the juices have run and the mushrooms are beginning to brown. Add the flour and stir well until the flour is cooked, about 2–3 minutes. Gradually add the stock or milk, stirring well to prevent lumps from forming. Pour the sauce over the fish and leek mixture. If you are using anchovies, arrange them on top of the sauce. Sprinkle the breadcrumbs over the top. Bake for 25 minutes. Serve sprinkled with parsley.

Below: Cloghane in winter.

RABBIT WITH ALMONDS

SERVES 4

Rabbit, enjoying a great revival, was immensely popular in the past. Dozens of recipes survive from Irish household recipe books. Almonds, too, were widely used for flavor and texture in a variety of dishes. Today's tender rabbits are specially bred for the table. Wild rabbits take rather longer to cook and have a gamier flavor.

2½–3 lb/1.15–1.3 kg rabbit, cut into 8–10 pieces

1 tablespoon vinegar

1 tablespoon salt

6 oz/175 g blanched whole almonds

salt and freshly ground black pepper

2 tablespoons all-purpose flour

2 tablespoons/30 g butter

1 tablespoon oil

2 onions, sliced

¼ lb/110 g streaky bacon, chopped

2 tablespoons Irish whiskey

a fresh thyme sprig

1 bay leaf

a glass of white wine

a glass of stock or water

grated zest and juice of 1 lemon

plain cooked rice, to serve

Soak the rabbit pieces for 1 hour in water, with the vinegar and salt. If the rabbit is wild, soak overnight. In a large frying pan, lightly brown the almonds with a teaspoon of oil.

Preheat the oven to 350°F/180°C.

Remove the rabbit pieces from the water, rinse well, and pat dry. Season the pieces and flour well. Brown the rabbit in the butter and oil in an ovenproof casserole dish. Add the onions and bacon and continue cooking until softened slightly. Add the whiskey, herbs, wine, stock or water, lemon juice and zest, and the almonds. Season to taste with salt and pepper.

Cover tightly and transfer to the oven and cook for about 1 hour. Test with a skewer and add a little more wine or stock if it needs more cooking or seems to be dry.

Serve the rabbit and almonds arranged on a dish of plain rice and pour the pan juices on top.

Opposite: Wildflower meadow.

RAGOUT OF COD AND CLAMS

SERVES 6

In the past, clams made only very occasional appearances on the western shores of Ireland, but in recent years they have been cultivated very successfully and have found a natural place in Irish cooking. Rice or baby potatoes, buttered and sprinkled with herbs, are good served with this.

2 large onions

1 tablespoon olive oil

2 garlic cloves

3 tablespoons balsamic vinegar

1¼ cups/300 ml fish or chicken stock

2 x 14 oz/400 g cans chopped Italian tomatoes

1 tablespoon chopped cilantro

salt and freshly ground black pepper

1½ lb/675 g cod fillet

1½ lb/675 g clams, scrubbed

basmati rice or baby potatoes with
    butter and herbs, to serve

Slice the onions into fine rings and put them in a heavy, flameproof casserole dish or saucepan with the oil and garlic. Sauté gently until they are soft but not brown, then add the balsamic vinegar and the stock. Cover and cook over moderate heat until the stock has almost evaporated and become slightly syrupy, but watch that it doesn't burn. This takes about 10-15 minutes.

Now add the tomatoes and cilantro and cook for a further 10 minutes to reduce slightly. Taste for seasoning. Cut the cod into large cubes and add the fish to the sauce, along with the clams, still in their shells. Cover and cook gently for 6-7 minutes until the cod is cooked and the clams have opened. Discard any clams that are still closed. Add a few grinds of black pepper and serve with rice or buttered potatoes.

SPICED BEEF

SERVES 6

Spiced beef is one of the seasonal pleasures of Christmas. Decorated with holly and embalmed in spices, it can be seen in every butcher's shop in Ireland during the Christmas season. To make it at home, you must start 8–10 days before serving. It sounds like a lot of work, but in fact it doesn't really take a lot of time once the ingredients are assembled. Remembering to attend to it each day is the difficult part.

4½ lb/2 kg beef brisket

FOR THE BRINE
¾ cup/225 g salt
1 teaspoon saltpeter (optional)
½ cup/110 g brown sugar
1¼ cups/300 ml Guinness
6½ cups/1.5 liters cold water

FOR THE SPICE MIX
2 teaspoons each ground black pepper, grated nutmeg, fresh thyme, and ground mace
1 teaspoon ground cloves
3 teaspoons allspice
2 bay leaves, crushed
1 onion, finely chopped

TO SERVE (OPTIONAL)
arugula
Dijon mustard
fruity chutney or cranberry sauce

In a good sized saucepan, combine the salt, saltpeter, brown sugar, and Guinness. Pour in the cold water, then bring slowly to a boil, turn down the heat, and simmer for 10 minutes. Turn off the heat and allow to cool fully. In a large non-reactive container (such as plastic, ceramic, glass, or stainless steel), cover the meat with the cooled brine and transfer to the fridge for 7 days, turning the meat in the brine every day.

Remove the meat from the brine, drain, and dry (discard the brine). Mix half of the spices with all of the onions and rub this mixture thoroughly into the meat. Divide the remaining spices into four portions. Wrap the meat in plastic wrap and return it to the fridge for another 3–4 days, turning and rubbing in more of the spice mixture each day, and basting with the liquid that has seeped out (top up the spice mixture if necessary).

Finally, return the meat to a clean saucepan, cover with cold water, slowly bring to a boil, lower the heat, and simmer gently for 3–3½ hours, checking with a skewer after 2¾ hours. Cool in the liquid before drying and wrapping in foil. Keep in the fridge for a week to 10 days. Any remaining spices can be rubbed into the meat before wrapping it in foil.

Serve the beef cold, finely sliced, and presented on a bed of arugula, with Dijon mustard and a good fruity chutney or cranberry sauce on the side. It can also be eaten hot, rather like ham.

Notes: The final cooking can be done in the oven if preferred. Bring to a boil as above, then transfer to the oven at 350°F/180°C, checking as above.

Saltpeter is not essential, rather it is used to preserve the color of the meat. it is available online or you can use Prague Powder number 1 (also known as curing salt), which can be purchased from a meat-curing butcher or specialty store.

VENISON PASTIES

SERVES 6

These small pasties are a manageable version of the great decorated venison pies of the past. These were "sideboard" dishes, which allowed the pastry cooks to show off their art. Widely available during the winter months, both farmed and wild, venison is a lean meat and benefits from a pre-cooking marinade, which should be as long as time allows.

2 lb/900 g breast of venison, or pieces

2 tablespoons olive oil

2 tablespoons red-wine vinegar

2 garlic cloves, crushed

1 teaspoon ground mace

6–7 juniper berries, slightly crushed

salt and freshly ground black pepper

2 large onions

1 carrot, peeled

1 celery stick

¼ lb/110 g chopped bacon

2 lb/900 g puff pastry

1 egg, beaten

Cut the venison into cubes and put them in an ovenproof dish with the oil, vinegar, crushed garlic, spices, and salt and pepper to taste. Leave overnight, if possible.

Preheat the oven to 325°F/160°C. Finely chop the vegetables. Fry the bacon cubes until crisp. Add the bacon and vegetables to the meat and marinade, cover, and bake for 45 minutes to 1 hour, or until the meat is just tender, but check once or twice because venison doesn't benefit from overcooking. Remove and cool.

Turn the oven up to 350°F/180°C.

Roll out the pastry to make 6 pieces, each about 6 x 8 inches/15 x 20 cm, patching holes together if necessary. Pour out and keep any excess gravy from the meat. Divide the meat among the pastry pieces, putting it in the center and leaving a gap of 2 inches/5 cm on either side and 1 inch/2.5 cm at the top and bottom. Dampen the edges with beaten egg and draw the sides together, pinching well. Pinch together the tops and bottoms securely. Line a baking sheet with parchment paper and lay the pasties on it, seam-side down, and poke a hole in the top of each one. Brush over with beaten egg, and decorate as lavishly as the pastry trimmings will allow.

Bake for about 20–30 minutes until the pastry is golden brown. The remaining gravy can be passed around separately, with a dash of lemon juice added. Rowan berry or redcurrant jelly is very good with venison.

BEEF AND MUSHROOM PIE WITH GUINNESS

SERVES 6

Beef shank is a great choice for slow cooking, for, although it takes a long time to cook initially, it remains tender and juicy.

2 lb/900 beef shank, trimmed and cubed

2 tablespoons all-purpose flour

2 tablespoons olive oil

1 bay leaf

1 fresh thyme spring

1 fresh parsley or sage sprig

2 large onions, chopped

1 carrot, chopped

1 celery stick, chopped

salt and freshly ground black pepper

4 canned anchovies, drained

2 cups/450 ml Guinness

½ lb/225 g mushrooms

½ lb/225 g puff pastry

1 egg, beaten

mashed potatoes or boiled baby potatoes, or crusty
    bread and salad, to serve

Toss the beef in the flour and brown in the oil in a large saucepan. Tie the bay leaf, thyme, and parsley to make a bouquet garni. Add the onions to the pan and toss about until they begin to soften, then add the carrot, celery, the bouquet garni, and seasoning. Mash the anchovies and stir them in. Pour the Guinness over the top, stir well, cover, and cook very gently until the meat is almost tender, about 1 ½ hours. (This can be done in the oven, if preferred.) Add the mushrooms and continue cooking for another 25 minutes. Allow the filling to cool.

Preheat the oven to 375°F/190°C.

Transfer the contents of the saucepan to a deep pie dish and check the seasoning. On a floured board, roll the pastry out into a large circle about 1 ½ inches/4 cm larger than the pie dish. Cut off the surplus 1 ½ inches/4 cm of pastry from around the edge of the circle in a long strip, and press this strip onto the dampened edge of the dish. Lay the remaining pastry circle (now the size of your dish) over the pie, pressing it onto the strip to attach it well and crimping the edges decoratively. Make a vent in the center and decorate the pie with leaves or flowers made from the pastry trimmings. Brush with the beaten egg and bake for about 35 minutes until the pastry is risen and golden.

Eat this with creamy mashed potatoes or boiled baby potatoes tossed in butter and parsley, or fresh crusty bread and a green salad.

BREAST OF CHICKEN WITH WALNUT AND APPLE

SERVES 4

"On rainy days alone I dine,
Upon a chick, and pint of wine.
On rainy days I dine alone,
And pick my chicken to the bone."

Jonathan Swift

toothpicks or cocktail sticks

4 tablespoons/55 g butter

½ large, tart cooking apple, peeled and chopped

4 fresh sage leaves, finely chopped, or a tiny pinch of dried sage

3 oz/75 g walnuts, chopped

salt and freshly ground black pepper

4 large chicken breasts

2 tablespoons all-purpose flour

1 egg, beaten

¾ cup/75 g breadcrumbs

1 tablespoon oil

generous ½ cup/150 ml heavy cream or crème fraîche

paprika, to taste

In a small pan, melt 1 tablespoon/15 g of the butter and add the apple, sage, and walnuts. Cook gently until the apple is just beginning to soften and the walnuts are beginning to color. Set aside to cool and season well.

Make a long, deep incision in the side of each chicken breast, cutting lengthways to make a deep pocket. Divide the stuffing among the chicken breasts, pushing it well into the pockets. (If you are preparing this dish in advance, chill the stuffing before inserting it.) Season and flour the chicken breasts, dip each one in egg, and then roll in breadcrumbs. Secure with cocktail sticks.

In a large pan, melt 2 tablespoons/30 g of the butter with the oil and fry the chicken gently, turning once or twice, until cooked and golden but still moist, about 5–7 minutes on each side, depending on thickness. Remove the chicken and keep warm. Wipe any burned crumbs from the pan with paper towel and pour in the cream. Add any remaining stuffing or crumbs, season well with salt, pepper, and paprika, and let it bubble up for a few moments, scraping up the sediment. Whisk in the remaining butter and pour the sauce over the chicken.

Opposite: Cliffs of Moher, County Clare.

STUFFED PORK CHOPS
WITH POTATO APPLE FRITTERS

SERVES 4

You will need cocktail sticks or poultry pins for this recipe.

4 pork loin chops, 1 inch/2.5 cm thick

1 tablespoon balsamic vinegar

grated zest and juice of 1 lemon

1 tablespoon Dijon mustard

chopped fresh parsley

about 1 cup/55 g whole-wheat breadcrumbs

finely chopped fresh thyme

3 tablespoons/40 g butter

1 tablespoon grated fresh ginger

1 eating apple, peeled and finely chopped

salt and freshly ground black pepper

1 egg, beaten

1 tablespoon oil

generous ½ cup/150 ml hard cider, white wine, or chicken stock

FOR THE FRITTERS

½ lb/225 g potato, grated

¼ lb/110 g apple, grated

scant ½ cup/55 g all-purpose flour

2 eggs

2 tablespoons cream

oil and butter, for shallow frying

salt

Make cuts in the fat along the edge of the chops at ½ inch/1 cm intervals (this helps the fat to cook and prevents the chops from curling up when heated). Make a horizontal incision in the side of each chop, to form a pocket. Mix the vinegar, lemon juice, and mustard together and toss the meat well in this mixture. Leave to marinate while you make the stuffing, or longer, if time allows.

Put the parsley in a bowl with the lemon zest, breadcrumbs, and thyme. Melt 1 tablespoon/15 g of the butter in a large pan and cook the ginger for a few moments, then add the apple and cook until soft. Stir in the breadcrumb mixture, season well, and bind with the beaten egg. Allow to cool.

Spoon the stuffing into the pockets in the chops and secure with cocktail sticks or poultry pins. Add half the remaining butter and the oil to the pan, turn up the heat, and brown the chops well on both sides. Add the cider, wine, or stock and the remaining marinade. Cover the pan, lower the heat, and simmer very gently until the chops are cooked to your liking—about 6–8 minutes, turning once or twice. Transfer the chops to a serving dish and keep warm.

Add the remaining butter to the pan, scrape up the residue, bubble for a few moments to reduce, check and adjust the seasoning, and pour over the chops. Keep the chops warm while you make the fritters.

Mix the potato and apples together with the flour. Bind with the eggs and cream and mix to a batter consistency. Fry a tablespoon at a time in hot oil and butter for 3–5 minutes until crisp and golden brown; drain on paper towel and sprinkle with salt before serving with the chops.

ROAST TURKEY WITH STUFFING

SERVES 8–10

This turkey has two stuffings and is semi-braised, to retain moisture. You can garnish this dish with bacon rolls and mini sausages, and serve with rowan berry or cranberry jelly. You will need a skewer or some kitchen twine.

12 lb/5.5 kg turkey
4 tablespoons/55 g butter
salt and freshly ground black pepper
2 large onions, halved
8 cloves
2 carrots, coarsely chopped
2 celery stalks, coarsely chopped
½ lb/225 g bacon strips
1¼ cups/300 ml hard cider or white wine

FOR THE PRUNE AND CHICKEN LIVER STUFFING

1 large onion, finely chopped
4 tablespoons/55 g butter
½ lb/225 g chicken livers, cleaned and chopped
about 3¼ cups/350 g fresh breadcrumbs
1 celery stick, finely chopped
1 carrot, grated
½ lb/225 g prunes, pitted and chopped
½ cup/125 ml vermouth or sherry
2 teaspoons dried mixed herbs (like herbes de Provence)
1 teaspoon ground mace

FOR THE APPLE AND WALNUT STUFFING

1 cup/175 g chopped walnuts
2 cooking apples, peeled and chopped
4 tablespoons/55 g butter, softened
1 tablespoon grated fresh root ginger
½ cup/55 g fresh breadcrumbs

Opposite: A peaceful night in County Sligo.

Preheat the oven to 450°F/230°C.

To make the prune stuffing, cook the onion in half the butter, then add the livers and cook until slightly pink. Place the breadcrumbs in a large bowl and stir in the onion mixture. In the remaining butter, cook the celery, carrot, and prunes for a few minutes, then add the vermouth or sherry, herbs, mace, and some salt and pepper. Let it bubble up well. Mix into the breadcrumb mixture and cool.

To make the apple stuffing, mix all the ingredients together and season well with salt and pepper.

Stuff the turkey's body cavity loosely with the prune stuffing (or it can be baked separately if preferred). Insert slices of butter under the breast skin. Skewer or tie the legs together. Stuff the crop with the apple stuffing and secure with a skewer. Season the turkey thoroughly and rub the breast well with butter. Put the halved onions, stuck with the cloves, in a deep roasting pan with the vegetables, bacon, and cider. Lay the turkey on its side on top.

Put the turkey in the oven and immediately lower the heat to 350°F/180°C. After 45 minutes, turn the turkey onto its other side and baste well. After a further 45 minutes, turn the turkey breast-side up and continue cooking for another 45 minutes to 1 hour, basting well and covering the breast with foil if it is browning too fast. Test by inserting a skewer between the thigh and the breast; the juices should run clear. Transfer the turkey to a platter and cover with foil and a dish towel; set the turkey aside to allow the meat to relax and the juices to be reabsorbed. It will stay warm for 45 minutes to 1 hour.

To make the gravy, strain the stock from the roasting pan and leave it to stand so the fat rises to the top. Remove the fat and set it aside. Mix 1 tablespoon of flour with 1 tablespoon of the fat in a saucepan, stir well, cooking for 2 minutes, then blend in the stock. Boil hard to reduce and thicken it slightly. Pour into a gravy boat and serve very hot.

SALADS AND SIDES

SALAD OF LAMB'S LETTUCE AND DANDELION GREENS

SERVES 6

Dandelions are thought to have great curative powers: true, or not, they make a great salad.

½ lb/225 g young dandelion greens

3 tablespoons wine or cider vinegar

½ lb/225 g lamb's lettuce (also known as corn salad)

6 streaky bacon strips

1 garlic clove, kept whole

salt and freshly ground black pepper

2–3 oz/55–75 g Cashel or other blue cheese

FOR THE VINAIGRETTE

1 teaspoon Dijon mustard

1 tablespoon cider or wine vinegar

salt and freshly ground black pepper

4–5 tablespoons olive oil

Wash the dandelion leaves and trim the stalks. Dry the leaves well, then put them in the salad bowl. Heat the vinegar and pour it over the dandelion greens; toss and leave for about 15 minutes (this helps to soften them). Pour out any surplus vinegar. Wash the lamb's lettuce and set aside to drain.

Meanwhile, make the vinaigrette: mix the mustard, vinegar, salt, and pepper together and whisk in the oil until smooth.

Fry the bacon in its own fat, with the garlic, until crisp. Remove the garlic and pour the bacon and pan juices over the dandelion leaves. Add the lamb's lettuce to the bowl and toss well with a little of the vinaigrette. Season to taste. Crumble the cheese on top and serve while the bacon is still warm, with any remaining dressing on the side.

Above right: Brandon Mountain, Dingle Peninsula, County Kerry.

Previous page: An old fishing boat on Lough Gill.

CHICKEN, ORANGE, AND ARUGULA SALAD WITH WALNUT SAUCE

SERVES 6

Large boneless, skinless chicken breasts,
    weighing about 1 lb/450 g in total

1¼ cups/300 ml chicken stock

salt

18–20 arugula leaves

2 large sweet oranges (3 if small)

FOR THE SAUCE

3 oz/90 g walnut halves

1 tablespoon cider or sherry vinegar, or more to taste

3 tablespoons walnut or olive oil

2 teaspoons sugar, or more to taste

1 garlic clove

Put the chicken in a saucepan and barely cover with the stock. Add a pinch of salt and poach gently until cooked but still moist, about 10–15 minutes. Remove the chicken and cool. Strain and reserve the stock. Shred the chicken by pulling it apart with 2 forks, lengthways, along the grain of the meat.

Wash and dry the arugula leaves and put them in the fridge to crisp.

To make the sauce, toast the walnuts in a dry pan until crisp and just beginning to brown. Put them in a blender with the other sauce ingredients and half the reserved stock. Grind to a smooth paste. Taste, adding more vinegar or sugar as you like. Use the remaining stock to dilute the sauce to the desired texture. Reserve 2 tablespoons of the sauce to finish.

Peel the oranges with a sharp knife, then slice down between the segments and separate the flesh from the dividing membrane. Allow 2 or 3 segments per person. All of this can be prepared ahead of time, or the day before.

To serve, pour a small pool of sauce on each plate, reserving 2 tablespoons. Arrange some of the chicken, topped with orange and arugula, on each plate. Thin the reserved 2 tablespoons of sauce with more stock or oil and drizzle over the top.

Opposite: Kells Bay Gardens in County Kerry.

PEAS AND LETTUCE

SERVES 6

This combination of two summer vegetables is more than 200 years old and, though its origins are French, it pops up frequently in old Irish recipe collections. No need to wait for summer. The frozen petit pois available in the freezer aisle are a great substitute for tender young summer peas. This dish is equally delicious with fish, chicken, or lamb.

1 lb/450 g petits pois, thawed, or small fresh peas

4 heads little gem lettuce

2 tablespoons/30 g butter

3–4 scallions, finely chopped

generous ½ cup/150 ml cream

chopped fresh chervil or basil

salt and freshly ground black pepper

Drain the peas well. Wash the lettuce and remove any damaged leaves. Cut each lettuce into eight lengthwise slices.

Melt the butter in a large frying pan or saucepan and gently cook the scallions. Add the peas, lettuce, cream, herbs, and seasonings. Cover for 5 minutes or so to soften the lettuce, but don't allow it to break up. Remove the lid and check the seasoning. Simmer gently for 8 minutes before serving.

ROAST BEEF SALAD

SERVES 6-8

A fillet of Irish beef needs few extras and is at its best simply prepared. For this summery salad, both the beef and sauce can be prepared well in advance.

FOR THE BEEF

1½ lb/675 g beef fillet, in one piece, trimmed and tied

4 tablespoons olive oil, plus extra for blending

2 tablespoons red wine vinegar

2 garlic cloves, crushed

2 teaspoons ground allspice

1 tablespoon Dijon mustard

FOR THE SALAD

2 bunches of scallions

mixed lettuce and herb leaves

cherry tomatoes

marigold petals or chive or arugula flowers (optional)

oil and vinegar or your favorite vinaigrette (optional)

FOR THE SAUCE

2 tablespoons white wine vinegar

1 teaspoon peppercorns

2 teaspoons each chopped fresh tarragon and parsley, mixed

4 egg yolks

1½ sticks/175 g unsalted butter, softened

Trim the meat of any fat and tie it around at intervals to keep its shape while cooking. Marinate the meat at room temperature in the oil, vinegar, and crushed garlic for 2-3 hours.

Preheat the oven to 425°F/220°C.

Remove the beef from the marinade and wipe dry with paper towel. Mix the allspice and mustard into a paste with a little oil and spread over the meat. Roast the meat for 20 minutes for pink beef, or cook for 5-7 minutes longer if preferred.

Five minutes before the end of the cooking time, brush the scallions with olive oil and scatter them over the meat. Remove the meat and set aside in a cool place to prevent further cooking.

To make the sauce, boil the vinegar, peppercorns, and 1 teaspoon of each of the herbs with ¼ cup/60 ml water until it has reduced to 2 tablespoons. Heat some water in a double-boiler, or a pan with a large heatproof bowl fitted on top. Strain the sauce into the double-boiler or bowl, and beat in the egg yolks. Stir well until the yolks are warm, then gradually stir in the softened butter, in walnut-sized lumps, stirring until the sauce thickens slightly and will coat the back of a spoon. Stir continuously, lifting the saucepan on and off the heat to prevent it from overheating and scrambling the eggs. When the sauce has thickened, pour it into a blender and whizz for a few moments until it becomes slightly foamy. Alternatively, whisk hard with a wire whisk. Add the remaining herbs, pour into a serving dish, cover, and set aside until needed.

Arrange the lettuce and herb leaves on a large serving dish. Untie the beef and slice very thinly. Arrange in an overlapping circle and put the leaves and wilted scallions in the center. Garnish with the tomatoes and whatever herb flowers you have on hand. If desired, dress the leaves with vinaigrette just before serving. Serve extra sauce separately.

Note: the beef will lose its pink color and darken if sliced too soon.

SAUTÉED CABBAGE
WITH BACON

SERVES 4

This dish is the perfect partner for fowl and game.

½ lb/225 g cubed bacon
2 tablespoons oil
2 tablespoons wine vinegar
1 teaspoon sugar
1 teaspoon caraway seeds
1¼ lb/550 g finely sliced or shredded cabbage,
    hard stalks removed
1 large cooking apple, peeled and chopped
salt and freshly ground black pepper

In a large pan, cook the bacon cubes in the oil until crisp. Remove and keep warm. Pour off the fat from the pan and add the vinegar, sugar, caraway seeds, and 6 tablespoons/90 ml water. Boil for a few moments, scraping up any sediment from the bottom of the pan.

Add the cabbage and apple to the pan and cook, turning frequently until the cabbage is just tender and the apple is soft and melting, about 7–8 minutes. Taste for seasoning, sprinkle the bacon on top, and serve.

Opposite: Fishing in Lough Gill.

COLCANNON

Though variations of Colcannon are eaten all year round, it is an essential part of the Halloween feast, when rings or coins, wrapped in paper and cooked into the dish, foretell marriage or riches to the lucky finders in the coming year.

1 lb/500 g kale or green cabbage
1½ lb/675 g potatoes, unpeeled
1 bunch scallions, finely chopped
¾ cup/175 ml hot cream or milk
1 stick/110 g butter
salt and white pepper

Remove the hard stalks from the kale or cabbage, and cook in salted, boiling water until tender. (Kale takes a surprisingly long time, about 25 minutes; cabbage will take 8–10 minutes.) Drain, press out any remaining water, and finely chop, by hand or using a food processor.

Boil the potatoes in salted water until soft. Peel and mash carefully by hand, removing any lumps (don't use the food processor for this or the potatoes will turn into glue).

The scallions can be cooked in the cream or milk for a few minutes, though personally I prefer them raw. Add them to the potatoes with the hot cream or milk, half the butter, and the kale or cabbage. Beat thoroughly together, adjust the seasoning, then turn out into a large serving bowl. Make a well in the center, and drop in the remaining butter in one piece. Serve very hot.

COLCANNON–A WEXFORD VERSION

SERVES 4

Almost every region of Ireland has its take on colcannon and each claims theirs as the "true" recipe. Like traditional dishes worldwide, the local version contains whatever is readily available in that region. Wexford's comfortable farms are known for their vegetable gardens and orchards.

8 potatoes
1 large parsnip
1 large onion
1 lb/450 g cabbage or kale
a bunch of fresh parsley, chopped
salt and freshly ground black pepper
1 stick/110 g butter
hot milk
chopped fresh parsley or scallions, to garnish

Peel the potatoes and boil with a little salt until soft. Wash, dry, and chop all the vegetables into small pieces, keeping one large cabbage or kale leaf aside. Place the vegetables in a steamer or colander over boiling water. Cover with the large kale or cabbage leaf and the lid and steam for 30 minutes to 1 hour until all the vegetables are tender and cooked to your liking.

Mash the potatoes, vegetables, and parsley together. Season with salt and pepper and add 5 tablespoons/75 g of the butter. Gradually add enough hot milk to make it creamy. Serve in a mound in a deep dish with the remaining butter pressed into the center and chopped parsley or scallions scattered over the top.

Opposite: Trees at the edge of Lough Gill.

GRATIN OF PARSNIPS AND PEARS

SERVES 6

"Fair words butter no parsnips"
Old saying

This is a simple and delicious parsnip dish that can be prepared a day in advance, put in the fridge, and finished when ready to cook. It is excellent with roast dinners of all sorts and it is particularly good with golden sausages.

3–4 large parsnips
3 large pears
salt and freshly ground black pepper
1 tablespoon lemon juice
4 tablespoons/55 g butter
grated nutmeg
¼ cup/30 g stale breadcrumbs, tossed in melted butter

Preheat the oven to 350°F/180°C.

Cut the parsnips into quarters, lengthways, and cut away some of the hard core, then peel, trim, and cut into chunks. Peel and core the pears and roughly chop. Put the parsnips and pears in a large saucepan. Add a little salt and the lemon juice and just barely cover with water. Simmer gently until tender. Drain well and mash thoroughly with the butter until smooth and creamy, adding black pepper to taste and a good grating of nutmeg.

Transfer to an oven dish and sprinkle the breadcrumbs over the top. Bake for 15–20 minutes, or until golden brown.

ORANGE, CELERY, AND WATERCRESS SALAD

SERVES 6

This winter salad is the classic partner for wild duck, but just as good with tame fowl or pork. Lamb's lettuce (also called corn lettuce) or arugula can be used instead of the watercress.

2–3 oranges

1–2 bunches of watercress

6–8 celery stalks, finely sliced

1 small onion, finely chopped

2 tablespoons olive oil

1 tablespoon lemon juice

salt and paprika

Peel the oranges, removing as much pith as possible. Wash and gently shake the watercress dry. Arrange the watercress leaves on a flat dish with the celery. Slice the oranges into thin rounds and arrange on top, removing any seeds. Sprinkle the finely chopped onion over the oranges and season with salt.

Dress the salad with oil and lemon just before serving and sprinkle a little paprika over the top.

Below: *Calm reflections in Caragh Lake.*

DESSERTS

ORANGE CREAMS

SERVES 4

Seville oranges, both zest and pith, were used to make these delicious creams in the past, when oranges were a seasonal commodity. One Seville orange, with its stronger flavor, would be sufficient.

2 unwaxed oranges

4 egg yolks

2 egg whites

generous ½ cup/150 ml cream

generous ½ cup/150 ml milk

about 2 tablespoons sugar, or to taste

1 tablespoon brandy, rum, or orange liqueur

small, skinned orange segments or more orange zest, for decoration (optional)

whipped cream, to serve

Scrub the orange skins well and then, with a potato peeler, peel the zest off, not too thinly (a very little pith will give more flavor). Squeeze the juice. Combine the orange zest, juice, and a little extra water in a small saucepan and simmer very gently until the zest is soft. This takes a surprisingly long time, perhaps 45 minutes, and you will probably need to add a few spoonfuls more water from time to time. When the zest is soft, allow the liquid to evaporate, being careful not to let it burn.

Preheat the oven to 300°F/150°C.

Purée the zest in a food chopper or with a mortar and pestle. Add the eggs, cream, and milk, sugar to taste, and the brandy, rum, or liqueur and pour the mixture into 4 buttered ramekins. A strip of zest or a small, skinned orange section can be gently laid on top of each to decorate.

Set the ramekins in water in a roasting pan and bake for about 35–40 minutes until set when tested with a knife. Refrigerate and serve cold, in the ramekins, with a spoonful of whipped cream on top.

Above and previous page: Coumeenoole Sands and Slea Head, Dingle Peninsula.

CINNAMON CUSTARD

SERVES 4

This is an ideal filling for pancakes and it also makes a wonderful filling for a sponge cake.

4 egg yolks
generous ½ cup/110 g sugar
scant ½ cup/55 g cornstarch
generous 2 cups/500 ml milk
½ cinnamon stick
1 vanilla pod

Mix the egg yolks with the sugar and cornstarch. Slowly bring the milk to a boil with the cinnamon stick and vanilla pod, then turn off the heat and leave to infuse for 15 minutes.

Remove the cinnamon and vanilla. Bring the milk back to a boil and pour into to the egg mixture, stirring rapidly. Return the mixture to the saucepan over low heat, and stir continuously until the mixture thickens slightly. Do not allow it to boil, or the eggs will scramble. Pour into a shallow bowl to cool.

Note: If serving with pancakes, spread the pancakes with a few spoonfuls of the custard, sprinkle with a few drops of brandy, and roll up. Reheat in a moderate oven (350°F/180°C), for 15 minutes.

PANCAKES

SERVES 4

These thin, crêpe-like pancakes are traditionally eaten on Shrove Tuesday, the day before Lent begins. Shrove Tuesday pancakes are served in the simplest manner, with sugar, lemon juice, and butter, and it's hard to improve on this. However, for a simple and delicious dessert, fill them with Cinnamon Custard.

generous 1½ cups/225 g all-purpose flour
1 tablespoon sugar
a pinch of ground ginger or grated nutmeg
2 eggs, beaten
4 tablespoons/55 g butter, melted
2½ cups/600 ml milk
oil and melted butter, for frying
custard and seasonal fruits, to serve (optional)

Mix the dry ingredients together and then add the eggs, butter, and milk. Beat thoroughly and set aside for at least an hour to let the flour expand.

Heat a heavy 7 inch/18 cm frying pan until hot and add a teaspoon each of oil and butter. Swirl it around the pan and pour the surplus into a little dish. Pour a small ladleful of batter into the pan and swirl it around to form a thin skin. Cook until golden brown, then turn with a palette knife and cook for a few moments longer. (The first couple of pancakes invariably break up or stick.) Dip a pastry brush in oil and melted butter and brush the pan again before cooking each pancake. Stack, placing a sheet of wax paper between each pancake. They can be reheated gently in the oven or microwave. Serve with custard and seasonal fruits, if you like.

Note: Don't use a nylon pastry brush—it will melt. A twist of paper towel works well also.

STRAWBERRIES IN CLARET JELLY

SERVES 6

Eating strawberries with red wine is a very old custom, the acidity of both being tempered by the liberal use of sugar and spices. Choose a wine you would like to drink and think of the poet Keats:

"How I like Claret! When I can get Claret, I must drink it....

If you could make some wine like Claret to drink on summer evenings in an arbour ..."

John Keats, letter to his brother, 1819

¾ lb/350 g strawberries

2½ cups/600 ml claret or other red wine

8 teaspoons or 2 x ½ oz/11 g envelopes or 6 leaves gelatine

¾ cup/200 g redcurrant jelly

generous ½ cup/110 g sugar, or to taste

1 cinnamon stick

2–3 tablespoons water

2 tablespoons brandy

2 tablespoons lemon juice

strawberries and fruits, to decorate

whipped cream infused with scented
    geranium leaves, to serve

Wipe the strawberries with paper towel, and hull them. Put 3–4 tablespoons of the wine in a small bowl and sprinkle the gelatine over it. When the gelatine has softened, stand the bowl in hot water and stir until the gelatine has completely dissolved. Keep warm.

Heat the redcurrant jelly, sugar, and cinnamon stick in a saucepan with the water until both sugar and jelly have dissolved. Taste (you may like more sugar). Remove the cinnamon and strain the liquid into a large bowl. Add the gelatine and mix thoroughly, making sure there are no little undissolved globules of gelatine. When cool, add the remaining wine, along with the brandy and lemon juice.

Pour half the mixture and half the strawberries into a dampened 5 cup/1.2 liter jelly mold and allow it to set in the refrigerator. Warm the remaining jelly mixture, add the rest of the strawberries, and fill up the mold. (If this operation is done all at once, the strawberries will float to the top.) Once completely set, turn it out onto a platter and decorate with fruits, flowers, and leaves.

Have a bowl of whipped cream at hand, for those who like it. A couple of scented geranium leaves, infused in the whipped cream for an hour or so, give a subtle flavor.

Opposite: Upper Lake, Count Kerry.

CHERRY MOUSSE

SERVES 6

1 lb/450 g cherries

1 tablespoon each grated lemon zest and lemon juice

4 teaspoons or 1 x ½ oz/11 g envelope or 3 leaves gelatine

4 eggs

¼ cup/55 g sugar

generous ½ cup/150 ml whipping cream

summer fruits or fresh mint leaves, to decorate

Poach the cherries in as little water as possible until soft enough to extract the pits, then drain, reserving any cooking liquid. Purée the cherries with 1–2 tablespoons of the cooking water and the lemon zest and juice. Use the remaining cooking water to dissolve the gelatine, topping it up with water according to the directions on the package. Set aside to cool.

Separate the eggs and place the yolks and sugar in a heatproof bowl over a pan of hot water. Whisk over low heat until thick and creamy. Remove from the heat and whisk from time to time until cool. Stir the gelatine mixture thoroughly into the egg mixture, then beat in the cherry purée. Lightly whip the cream and fold it in.

Whisk the egg whites to the soft-peak stage and, when the gelatine mixture is just at the point of setting, fold the whites in carefully, amalgamating them thoroughly. Divide the mousse among 6 ring molds or ramekins and allow them to set in the refrigerator. Decorate with berries or mint leaves.

ROSE-PETAL ICE CREAM

SERVES 4

Scented roses are one of the great pleasures of summer. Make the most of them with this romantic ice cream. You can buy rose water at South Asian or Middle Eastern grocery stores, delicatessens, and major supermarkets. Make sure your rose petals are free of pesticides.

2½ cups/600 ml organic red or pink scented rose petals

generous ½ cup/110 g sugar

generous ½ cup/150 ml rosé wine

5 egg yolks

1 vanilla pod or 1 teaspoon vanilla extract

1¼ cups/300 ml milk

1¼ cups/300 ml heavy cream

½–1 teaspoon rose water

crystallized rose petals, to decorate (see note)

To prepare the rose petals, wipe them clean with damp paper towel and cut away the hard white stem or heel. Put them in a blender or food processor, with half of the sugar and the wine, and purée.

Beat the eggs and remaining sugar thoroughly. Split the vanilla pod, if using, and add to the milk and cream in a small pan. Bring to a boil and simmer gently for a few moments to infuse, then remove the pod. Add vanilla extract now, if using. Pour the hot mixture slowly into the eggs and sugar and return to the saucepan, stirring continuously. Heat to just below boiling point, but don't let it boil. The point is reached when the mixture coats the back of a spoon. Leave to cool.

Once cool, mix in the rose purée and rose water, a drop at a time. Taste for sweetness. Freeze in the usual way, stirring and beating it 2 or 3 times during the freezing process or use an ice cream maker. To serve, decorate with crystallized rose petals.

Note: To make crystallized rose petals, wipe and trim the petals as for the ice cream. Beat one large egg white until just fluid. Dip each petal into the egg white and then dredge in superfine sugar, covering it completely. Cover a baking sheet with parchment paper, then spread the petals on it and dry in a very low oven, with the door ajar, for an hour or so until they are crisp. Store in an airtight container between sheets of wax paper. They are great for cake decoration, too.

Opposite: Blennerville Village, Tralee.

SYLLABUS

SERVES 4

In the seventeenth century, this was a popular confection. It was made with wine, cider, or fruit juice, to which milk was added with force—often by milking the cow directly into the other ingredients—to make froth, or bubbles, hence the name "silly bubbles." It was also the traditional covering for trifle before whipped cream became universal.

1 ¼ cups/300 ml whipping cream
3 tablespoons sweet white wine or sherry (not dry)
juice of ½ orange
grated zest of ½ lemon
¼ cup/55 g superfine sugar

TO DECORATE
seasonal berries
Macaroons (see page 158)

Whip all the ingredients together until thick and creamy and the mixture will just hold its shape. Carefully spoon into four stemmed glasses. Make the syllabub a few hours in advance to allow the flavors to develop. Garnish with berries and serve with macaroons.

Left: Waterfall at Kell's Bay Gardens.

AUTUMN PUDDING

SERVES 4–5

This is an autumnal version of the classic Irish summer pudding. It is a sort of consolation for the passing of the brilliant summer raspberries and redcurrants. In its own way, it's just as nice.

The traditional combination is apples, plums (peeled, pitted, and cubed), and blackberries. The bread should be stale, at least two days old, and anything from sandwich bread to brioche is suitable if it can be cut to shape. Leftover Barm Brack (see page 160) is excellent. Homemade custard, hot or cold, or whipped cream mixed with crème fraîche are equally good on the side.

2 lb/900 g mixed fruit, like apples, plums, blackberries, and rhubarb
sugar, to taste (optional)
a little butter, for greasing
8–10 slices stale bread
custard or whipped cream, to serve (optional)

Cook the fruit gently in a saucepan, using as little water as possible to moisten it (1–2 tablespoons at most) or, better still, cook it in the microwave until just soft and the juice is just beginning to run. Sweeten to taste. Strain and reserve a few tablespoonfuls of the juice.

Butter a 7 cup/1.75 liter pudding basin or heavy mixing bowl. Cut a round from one slice of bread to fit the bottom of the bowl, then cut the rest into sections to fit the sides, reserving some for the top. Dip one side of each slice in the reserved juice, then use it to line the bowl, soaked-side out. Gently spoon in the cooled fruit, arrange the top pieces of bread to fit tightly, then cover with parchment paper or foil. Put a small plate or saucer on top and weigh it down with a tin can so that the juice will seep into the bread. Keep any juice that spills over. Allow the fruit to cool, then refrigerate overnight.

To serve, run a knife around the edge between the bread and the bowl and turn out on to a deep plate. Pour any remaining juice over the top. Serve with custard or whipped cream, if you like.

Overleaf: Caragh Lake.

A GREEN FOOL

The creamy, unctuous qualities of the avocado are not often used in sweet dishes. Combined here with the last of the summer gooseberries, it brings a new twist to the classic gooseberry fool.

1½ lb/675 g gooseberries
1 large, ripe avocado
zest and juice of 1 lime
sugar
langues de chats (see below), macaroons (p. 158), or other cookies, to serve

Wash the gooseberries, snip off the stems and flower ends, and cook the berries until they are soft and the juice runs. This can be done in the oven or gently on the stove, but the microwave is ideal because the berries seem to keep their color. Purée the gooseberries in a food processor and then pass through a sieve to remove the seeds.

Peel the avocado, remove the stone, chop the flesh, and immediately toss it with a little of the lime juice.

Return the gooseberry purée to the processor, add the avocado, and blend until creamy. Sweeten the purée to your taste with the sugar, add the lime zest, and the juice of half the lime. Chill for at least an hour. Serve in glasses, with pretty cookies or macaroons.

Note: To make *langues de chats*, or cats' tongues cookies, cream together 6 tablespoons/75 g butter and 6 tablespoons/75 g sugar until pale and creamy, then mix in 3 unbeaten egg whites. Fold in ½ cup/75 g all-purpose flour, then pipe 2 inch/5 cm strips of the mixture on lined baking sheets and bake in a preheated oven at 400°F/200°C for 6–8 minutes until golden brown around the edges. Using a spatula, carefully transfer to a wire rack to cool.

PEARS POACHED IN WHITE WINE

generous ½ cup/110 g sugar
2 cinnamon sticks
grated zest of 1 small orange
a bottle of sweet white wine, e.g. Muscatel or similar
6 pears
1 tablespoon lemon juice
grated nutmeg, to decorate

Put the sugar, cinnamon sticks, orange zest, and wine in a saucepan just large enough to hold the pears upright. Heat the liquid gently until the sugar dissolves, and then boil hard for a few minutes to create a light syrup.

Peel the pears carefully, leaving the stalks on, and brush them with lemon juice. Trim the bottoms slightly, so they will stand upright. If there is insufficient liquid to come up to the stalks, add water. Poach in the wine for about 15 minutes, or until they are tender but not too soft. When the pears are cooked, remove and cool.

Take the cinnamon sticks out of the poaching liquid and boil the liquid hard, uncovered, until it forms a thin syrup. Leave to cool. Pour the syrup over the pears and grate a little nutmeg over the top just before serving.

Right: Blarney Castle, Cork.

QUEEN OF PUDDINGS

SERVES 6

Here is a lighter version of the perennial favorite, which seems to please young and old alike.

5 eggs
2 cups/450 ml cream
1¼ cups/300 ml milk
1 teaspoon lemon zest
a small piece of cinnamon stick
½ teaspoon vanilla extract
1 cup/200 g sugar
¾ cup/75 g fresh breadcrumbs
4–5 tablespoons raspberry jam

Separate 3 of the eggs and set the whites aside for the meringue. Beat the remaining eggs and yolks together with the cream, milk, zest, cinnamon, vanilla, and 2 tablespoons of the sugar. Put the breadcrumbs in an ovenproof dish, pour the cream mixture over them, and set aside for an hour or two to allow the crumbs to swell.

Preheat the oven to 325°F/160°C.

Bake the dish for 15–20 minutes until set. Allow to cool for a few minutes, then spread the jam over the surface. Raise the heat to 375°F/190°C.

Beat the egg whites until they form stiff peaks. Slowly sprinkle in half of the remaining sugar, whisking continuously, and then fold in the remaining sugar thoroughly.

Evenly spread the egg white mixture over the jam layer and bake for 15 minutes until the meringue is just set and slightly brown, keeping an eye on it so it doesn't burn.

CHRISTMAS PUDDING

SERVES 6

This dense boiled fruitcake is a staple in Ireland for Christmas. While today's taste is for lighter food, an exception is always made in favor of the traditional Christmas pudding, although it, too, is evolving—butter is widely used today instead of suet and there hasn't been any meat in it for almost a hundred years. You will need two 3½ cup/850 ml pudding basins or heatproof mixing bowls.

6 oz/175 g candied cherries

½ lb/225 g candied citrus peel

3 oz/75 g each walnuts and blanched almonds

3¼ cups/350 g breadcrumbs

scant ½ cup/55 g all-purpose flour

1 cup/225 g light brown sugar

1 large apple, peeled and chopped

½ lb/225 g each raisins, currants, and golden raisins

1 tablespoon ground pumpkin pie spice

pinch of salt

3 sticks/350 g butter or shredded suet

8 eggs

a large glass of Irish whiskey or sherry

¾ cup/175 ml Guinness

Cut the cherries into halves. Thinly slice the candied peel and then chop it finely. Coarsley chop the nuts. Mix all the fruit together with the breadcrumbs, flour, sugar, apple, dried fruit, spice, and a pinch of salt. Place the butter (softened) or suet in another bowl, and gradually beat in the eggs and the whiskey or sherry. Pour this mixture into the dry ingredients and mix well. Add enough of the Guinness to give a dropping texture, but don't make it too runny.

Place discs of parchment paper in the bottoms of two 3½ cup/850 ml pudding basins or ovensafe mixing bowls and butter them well. Fill the bowls two-thirds full, leaving room for expansion. Cover the tops with more buttered paper, cut to size, and then cover well with foil. The puddings will need to steam for 5–6 hours: Choose a saucepan that will fit the bowl comfortably. Place a small trivet or rack in the bottom and stand the bowl on top. Fill the saucepan with boiling water to about 2 inches from the top of the bowl, replace the lid, and boil gently, topping up with boiling water as required. (The puddings can also be cooked at low heat in the oven, standing the bowls in a pan of water and enclosing both pan and bowl completely in foil, making a sort of steam-proof tent, for 5–6 hours at 300°F/150°C.) When cooked, allow to cool before removing the foil.

Cover with fresh parchment paper and more foil before storing in the refrigerator until required (up to a month). The puddings will require a further steaming of 1½–2 hours before they are served.

Note: the puddings can be left overnight in the refrigerator before cooking if it's not convenient to cook them immediately.

CINNAMON TOAST

MAKE 2 SLICES PER PERSON

A tea-time treat for children of all ages.

thick slices of white bread
butter
ground cinnamon
light brown sugar

Toast one side of the bread. Butter the untoasted side generously, sprinkle liberally with the cinnamon, and then the sugar. Toast under the broiler or in a toaster oven and eat immediately, while the buttery cinnamon runs down your chin.

A BOWL OF BISHOP

MAKES ABOUT 8 GLASSES

This was the favorite "nightcap" of the eighteenth century, famed in song and verse. Jonathan Swift wrote about it, though when his friend Stella made it for him, the oranges were roasted in front of the fire, and the wine heated with a hot poker.

4 oranges
20 cloves
1 cinnamon stick
1 teaspoon allspice berries
1 whole nutmeg
2–3 pieces of whole or blade mace (or use another nutmeg or more allspice)
a bottle of ruby port
sugar lumps or granulated sugar, to taste
juice of 1 lemon

Preheat the oven to 350°F/180°C.

Make incisions in 2 of the oranges, press the cloves into them, and roast for half an hour or so until they make a soft hissing sound.

In a saucepan, combine the whole spices with 2½ cups/600 ml water and boil until it has reduced by half. In another saucepan, gently heat the port, then ignite it to burn off some of the alcohol and concentrate the flavor. (If you don't feel like doing this part, ignore it!)

Put the port, spice water, and roasted oranges into a large bowl, ideally one that can be kept warm, and add sugar to taste. Slice the remaining 2 oranges and add them to the bowl, grate in some more nutmeg, and sharpen the flavor with lemon juice.

BAKING

IRISH CURD TART

SERVES 6

The ancient poetry of Gaelic Ireland has many images of feasting on rich curds, and these tarts are still enjoyed today. You will need pie weights.

1 lb/450 g cottage cheese
juice and grated zest of 1 lemon
2 tablespoons sugar, plus a little extra
½ cup/55 g almond meal
4 eggs
2 tablespoons raisins
grated nutmeg
whipped cream, to serve (optional)

FOR THE PASTRY
6 tablespoons/75 g butter
1 cup/140 g all-purpose flour
1 tablespoon sugar
1 egg yolk, beaten
1–2 tablespoons very cold water

Make the pastry in the usual way, by rubbing the butter into the flour and sugar and moistening with the egg yolk and 1–2 tablespoons of water, as required. Roll out to fit a greased 8 inch/20 cm tart pan and chill for 30 minutes.

Preheat the oven to 350°F/180°C. Cover the pastry with parchment paper or foil, fill with pie weights, and bake for 10 minutes. Remove the paper and weights and bake for a further 5 minutes until just golden. Set aside while you make the filling.

Blend or sieve the cottage cheese, lemon zest, sugar, and almond meal. Sharpen to taste by adding a little lemon juice. Beat the eggs, then fold thoroughly, with the raisins, into the cheese mixture. Pour into the prepared pastry and sprinkle a little sugar and grated nutmeg over the top. Bake for 30–40 minutes until golden brown. The mixture will gently subside as it cools.

Serve warm or cold. A little whipped cream is good with it, if it's to be served warm.

Note: the raisins can be soaked in a spoonful of whiskey for a few hours first, to plump them up and give a little extra flavor.

Overleaf: Winter snows across Glencar, County Kerry.

SIMNEL CAKE

SERVES 8–10

The simnel cake has been associated with Easter since medieval times and it must have been a delicious, spicy treat after the 40 days of the Lenten fast. Store-bought marzipan will speed up the preparation time. You can find golden syrup in British food stores or the international foods aisle of most supermarkets.

1 stick/110 g butter

5 tablespoons/75 g brown sugar

2 tablespoons golden syrup

4 large eggs

1¾ cups/250 g self-rising flour

1 teaspoon each ground cinnamon, grated nutmeg, and ground ginger

¾ lb/350 g mixed dried fruit

¼ lb/110 g candied citrus peel

1 tablespoon apricot jam, warmed

FOR THE MARZIPAN

1 lb/450 g ground almonds

1 cup and 2 tablespoons/225 g sugar

2 cups/225 g confectioners' sugar

2 eggs

2 teaspoons lemon juice

a few drops of almond extract

To make the marzipan, sift the almonds with the sugars. Beat the eggs, lemon juice, and almond extract together and stir into the almond mixture, kneading well until a smooth paste is formed. Break off eleven walnut-sized pieces, roll them into balls, and set aside (these were said to represent the twelve apostles of Jesus, minus Judas). Divide the remaining piece of paste in two and roll into two rounds that will fit the cake pan. Cover in plastic wrap and set aside.

To make the cake, preheat the oven to 325°F/160°C and grease and line an 8 inch/20 cm cake pan. Cream the butter, sugar, and syrup together. Add the eggs, beating well after each addition. Sift the flour and spices together, then fold into the egg mixture thoroughly. Fold in the fruit and candied peel.

Place half the mixture in the prepared pan and gently cover with a layer of marzipan. Layer the remaining mixture on top. Bake for 1 hour, then cover with a piece of foil, reduce the heat to 300°F/150°C, and cook for a further 30 minutes. Test with a skewer, which should come out clean, but remember not to push it down into the marzipan layer. When cooked, transfer to a wire rack and allow to cool for an hour or so. Remove from the pan and continue cooling.

When the cake is firm (after about half an hour), spread the apricot jam over the top of the cake, then press the second marzipan round on top, fluting the edges decoratively. Put the cake under the broiler (not too close to the heat) for a few moments to toast the top. Watch it carefully, since it can burn quickly. Now dampen the marzipan balls and press them around the top of the cake. Lower the oven rack and return the cake to the broiler to toast the balls. Tie a wide yellow ribbon around the cake for a festive appearance.

CHOCOLATE CAKE WITH MOCHA FILLING

SERVES 8

This delicious chocolate cake is perfect for a luxurious afternoon tea or a dinner party dessert to celebrate St. Valentine's Day.

FOR THE CAKE

generous 1 ½ cups/225 g all-purpose flour

1 cup/75 g unsweetened cocoa powder

4 large eggs, separated

5 tablespoons sunflower or canola oil

1 cup/225 g raw natural cane sugar

FOR THE FROSTING

6 tablespoons/75 g butter

1 cup/4 oz confectioners' sugar, sifted

2 teaspoons instant coffee, dissolved in 1 tablespoon hot water

1 tablespoon rum

TO DECORATE

2 cups/450 ml heavy whipping cream

1 tablespoon sugar

6 oz/175 g good dark chocolate

Preheat the oven to 375°F/190°C and grease and line an 8 inch/20 cm cake pan.

Sift the flour and cocoa together. Beat the egg yolks, oil, and sugar together until pale and creamy. Fold in the flour and cocoa. Beat the egg whites to a soft, dropping consistency and fold carefully into the flour mixture. Pour into the prepared cake pan, making a depression in the center. Bake for about 45 minutes. Test the cake with a skewer; if it comes out clean, the cake is cooked.

Cool the cake in the pan for 10 minutes before turning it onto a cake rack. When cold, split the cake in half horizontally.

To make the frosting, beat the butter to a cream with the confectioners' sugar, then beat in the coffee solution and rum. Spread lavishly on the bottom layer and sandwich the cakes together. Any surplus frosting can go on the top of the cake.

Whip the cream with the sugar until soft. Reserving some of the cream for decoration, cover the entire cake. With a potato peeler, pare some large flakes of chocolate for the top of the cake, then grate the remainder. Cover the sides of the cake with the grated chocolate, using a palette knife. Pipe or spoon the reserved cream around the top and scatter the chocolate flakes in the center.

HOT CROSS BUNS

MAKES 12–14

Hot cross buns are synonymous with Easter in Ireland, though, in fact, they are now thought to predate Christianity. Whatever their origins, they are delicious, especially toasted with plenty of butter. They are incomparably better homemade and, with instant yeast, very easy to make.

1½ lb/675 g all-purpose flour

½ oz/15 g envelope instant dry yeast

2 teaspoons sugar

1 teaspoon salt

3 teaspoons ground pumpkin pie spice, or to taste

4 tablespoons/55 g butter

1¼ cups/300 ml warm milk

1 large egg, beaten

5 oz/140 g mixed dried fruit

2 oz/55 g candied citrus peel

½ cup/110 g sugar and 1¼ cups/300 ml water,
    boiled together to form a syrup

Mix together the flour, yeast, sugar, salt, and spice. Soften the butter in the warm milk and add the beaten egg. Make a well in the flour and pour in the liquid, drawing in the flour from the sides and kneading well until a pliable dough has formed (this can be done in a food processor or mixer). Knead in the fruit and peel. Cover the dough with plastic wrap and set aside in a warm, dry place to rise for an hour or so.

Knock the air out of the dough and knead again for a few moments. Divide into 12–14 pieces and shape into balls. Arrange these on oiled baking sheets, cover, and leave to rise for a further 20–30 minutes.

Mix 2 tablespoons of flour and 1 tablespoon of water together and use it to paint a cross on the top of each bun. Preheat the oven to 375°F/190°C. Bake for about 20 minutes (when done, they will sound hollow when tapped underneath). With a pastry brush, paint the buns with the syrup and return to the oven for 5 minutes to set.

WHOLE-WHEAT SCONES

MAKES 12 SCONES

Almost every Irish household has its own recipe for "brown scones."

½ teaspoon salt

3 teaspoons baking powder

1¼ cups/175 g all-purpose flour

2⅔ cups/400 g coarse whole-wheat flour

¼ cup/55 g brown sugar

6 tablespoons/75 g butter, plus more to serve

2 eggs

1 cup/240 ml milk

Preheat the oven to 425°F/220°C.

Sift the salt and baking powder with the white flour and mix thoroughly with the whole-wheat flour. Add the sugar and rub in the butter with your fingers. Beat the eggs and milk together. Reserve a tablespoon or so, and fold the rest quickly and very lightly into the flour, working it as little as possible. If necessary, add a little more milk to form a relaxed dough.

Roll out on a floured surface to 1 inch/2.5 cm thick and cut into rounds or squares. Brush the tops with the reserved milk and egg.

Bake for about 20 minutes, or until there is a hollow sound when the scones are tapped underneath. Serve warm, split and buttered.

Above: Derrynane and Kenmare Bay, Ring of Kerry.

STRAWBERRY CHOCOLATE ROLL

SERVES 6

Swiss rolls and jelly rolls are a favorite component of the Irish tea table. This strawberry-filled chocolate roll is rich enough for an elegant summer dinner party.

FOR THE CAKE

½ cup/75 g all-purpose flour

scant ½ cup/30 g cocoa powder

½ teaspoon baking powder

2 large eggs

generous ½ cup/110 g sugar

2 tablespoons hot water

confectioners' sugar, sifted, to decorate

FOR THE FILLING

1 cup/240 ml heavy cream

¼ cup/55 g superfine sugar

brandy or vanilla extract, to taste

1 lb/450 g strawberries, cleaned and hulled

Preheat the oven to 425°F/220°C.

Butter a 12 x 9 inch/30 x 23 cm jelly roll pan and line with parchment paper. Cut another piece of parchment the same size and have ready a dish towel, to be wrung out in hot water.

Sift the flour, cocoa, and baking powder together. Beat the eggs and sugar together until thick, white, and creamy. With a large metal spoon, fold in the flour mixture, cutting with the edge of the spoon and turning, rather than mixing. Finally, fold in the hot water. Pour into the pan, smooth with a palette knife, and bake for 7–10 minutes or until the mixture has slightly shrunk away from the sides (the sponge cake will dry out if overcooked).

Put the piece of parchment paper on the hot dish towel and sprinkle it with sugar. Turn the cake out onto the paper. Quickly trim the edges, then carefully peel away the paper. With the help of the hot dish towel, roll up the sponge on the long side, enclosing the paper inside. (The hot towel helps to prevent cracks forming in the sponge). Leave to cool.

Stiffly whip the cream with the sugar and brandy or vanilla extract. Roughly chop three-quarters of the strawberries, then fold them into the cream. Carefully unroll the chocolate roll, remove the paper, and spread the strawberry mixture on the cake. Roll up the cake around the filling, then sprinkle with a little confectioners' sugar. Decorate with the remaining strawberries.

AUTUMN APPLE TART

SERVES 6

Armagh in Northern Ireland has been renowned for more than 200 years for the quality of her apples. Serve this tart with whipped cream or crème fraîche.

FOR THE PASTRY

1¼ cups/175 g all-purpose flour

pinch of salt

2 tablespoons/30 g sugar

1 stick/110 g butter

1 egg yolk

1 tablespoon lemon juice

FOR THE FILLING

3 large, tart, cooking apples that will break down when cooked

1 tablespoon grated lemon zest and 1 tablespoon lemon juice

sugar, to taste

3 large red dessert apples that will hold their shape when cooked

1 tablespoon melted butter

2 tablespoons confectioners' sugar

To make the pastry, sift the flour with a pinch of salt. Stir in the sugar. Rub the butter into the flour and salt with your fingertips, or pulse in the food processor. Beat the egg yolk with the lemon juice and mix it in. Add a few drops of cold water, if required. Roll out or pat into a greased 9 inch/23 cm tart pan. Chill while you prepare the filling.

Peel, core, and roughly chop the cooking apples and cook gently until soft, adding a spoonful of water, if necessary. Press through a sieve or purée in a food processor and add the grated lemon zest. Sweeten to taste with sugar and chill in the refrigerator. When cold, spread over the bottom of the pastry.

Preheat the oven to 375°F/190°C.

Quarter and core the unpeeled red apples, cut into neat slices, and brush with lemon juice. Arrange the slices in a circle around the pan, on top of the purée, covering it completely. Brush the slices with melted butter and then use a sieve to sprinkle a little confectioners' sugar over the top.

Cover the apple slices with a circle of foil and bake for about 15 minutes, then remove the foil and continue to bake for a further 20 minutes until the pastry has shrunk a little from the sides of the pan and the apples are slightly tinged with color. Serve warm or cold. Pass around whipped cream or crème fraîche separately.

APPLE DUMPLINGS

SERVES 6

"Coleridge holds that a man cannot have a pure mind who refuses apple dumplings. I am not certain but he is right."

Charles Lamb, The Essays of Elia

6 large dessert apples (such as Honeycrisp or Orin)

2 tablespoons lemon juice

5 sticks of rhubarb or 1 lb/450 g plums, pitted, or a mixture of both

2 tablespoons golden raisins

4 tablespoons/55 g butter

¾ cup/5 oz granulated raw cane sugar (such as turbinado), or to taste

6 cloves

1½ lb/675 g shortcrust or puff pastry, homemade or store bought

1 egg, beaten

ice cream, to serve

Preheat the oven to 350°F/180°C.

Peel the apples and brush with lemon juice. Remove the cores, then remove and reserve a little more apple from the centers to enlarge the cavities. Wash and chop the rhubarb or plums, add the removed apple pieces and the raisins, and cook gently in 2 tablespoons/30 g butter until soft but not mushy (a few minutes in a microwave is ideal). Fill the cored apples with the fruit mixture, sweeten to taste, reserving a tablespoon of sugar for sprinkling, and add a clove to each. Top with a pat of butter.

Cut the pastry into 6 pieces and roll them out to fit the apples. Set each apple on a square of pastry and dampen the edges. Draw up the corners, cut away the surplus pastry, and press the edges well together, molding the dough to encase the apples. Roll out the pastry trimmings to make leaves and use these to cover any imperfections. Make steam holes in the top of the pastry, brush with the beaten egg, and then sprinkle with the rest of the sugar.

Bake for about 45 minutes until the pastry is golden brown. Very large apples may take a little longer. A skewer pressed into the side will tell if they are done. Vanilla ice cream is very good indeed with apple dumplings.

Note: cooking apples can be used for apple dumplings if you like very tart flavors, but add extra sugar.

MARBLE CAKE

SERVES 6–8

Marble cake has fascinated children for generations and it is always a popular feature of the teatime spread.

scant 1 ½ cups/200 g all-purpose flour

1 teaspoon baking powder

salt

3 oz/75 g good dark chocolate (or 1 tablespoon cocoa powder
mixed with 2 tablespoons milk)

1 ½ sticks/175 g butter

generous ¾ cup/175 g sugar

3 large eggs

grated zest and juice of a small orange

Preheat the oven to 350°F/180°C. Butter and line an 8 cup/900 g loaf pan (about 9 x 5 x 3 inches/23 x 13 x 8 cm).

Sift the flour with the baking powder and a pinch of salt. Melt the chocolate, if using, in a double-boiler, microwave, or a heatproof bowl placed over a pan of hot water. Beat the butter in a large bowl until soft, then add the sugar and continue beating until the mixture is pale and creamy. Add the eggs, one by one, adding a spoonful of flour and beating well after each egg. Fold in the remaining flour carefully in a couple of batches, making sure no pockets of flour remain. Transfer half of the mixture to another bowl and add the orange zest and 1–2 tablespoons juice. Mix the chocolate or cocoa mixture gently but thoroughly into the first bowl.

Layer the mixtures into the prepared loaf pan, 3 spoonfuls of one and then the other, until you have used all the batter. Finally, draw a knife through the mixture diagonally from each end of the pan to create a marbled effect.

Bake for 45 minutes, or until the cake has shrunk slightly from the sides of the pan. Cover with foil if the top is browning too quickly. Leave to cool briefly in the pan, then transfer to a wire rack.

Below: Killorglin and River Laune, Ring of Kerry.

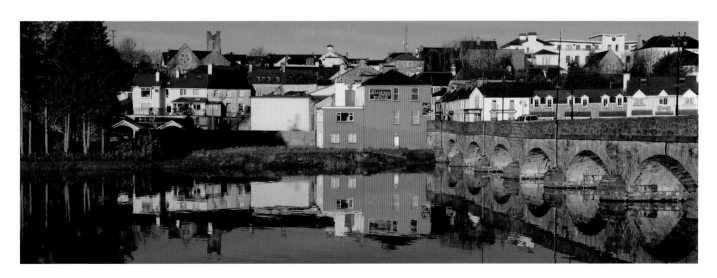

LONGFORD CAKES

MAKES 6 LARGE OR 12 SMALL TARTS

These delicious mouthfuls are simple to make for afternoon tea. Made larger, in 4 inch/10 cm tart pans, they make a good dessert, served with a little ice cream or the geranium-scented whipped cream alongside.

FOR THE PASTRY

2 cups/280 g all-purpose flour, sifted

1 tablespoon sugar

pinch of salt

1½ sticks/175 g butter

2 egg yolks

1–2 tablespoons cold water

FOR THE FILLING

2 tablespoons ground almonds

5 tablespoons apricot jam (finely chop any large chunks)

3½ oz/100 g walnuts, chopped

5 tablespoons raisins or golden raisins

2 tablespoons very finely chopped apple

1 tablespoon grated lemon zest

1 egg, beaten, to glaze

sugar, to decorate

FOR THE GERANIUM CREAM

1 cup/240 ml heavy or whipping cream

2–3 scented geranium leaves, washed and dried

To make the pastry, mix together the flour, sugar, and a pinch of salt. Rub in the butter, and then moisten with the egg yolks, adding a tablespoon or so of cold water as required. Chill for 30 minutes.

Preheat the oven to 375°F/190°C. For the larger version, grease and line six 4 inch/10 cm tartlet pans; for smaller cakes, use a well-buttered muffin pan. Roll out the pastry very thinly and line the pans, gathering the trimmings and re-rolling to make the lids.

Mix all the filling ingredients together and divide among the tarts. Dampen the pastry edges and put on the lids, press well together to seal and tidy up the edges. Glaze with the beaten egg, make vents in the tops, and sprinkle with sugar. Bake for 25–30 minutes until the pastry is golden brown.

To make the geranium cream, softly whip the cream, then infuse the leaves in the cream for several hours. Serve with the cakes.

ORANGE CARAWAY CAKE

SERVES 6–8

Caraway seeds were immensely popular in Irish cooking at least as far back as the seventeenth century and are just as popular today. This variation on the seed or Madeira cake is very good. Without the orange and marmalade, this makes an excellent plain seed cake, always on hand to offer with a glass of sherry or Madeira when friends come to call.

generous 1½ cups/225 g all-purpose flour

1¼ teaspoons baking powder

pinch of salt

1 stick/110 g butter

½ cup/110 g light brown sugar

2 large eggs

2 tablespoons fine cut marmalade

1 tablespoon caraway seeds

grated zest and juice of 1 orange

2 tablespoons confectioners' sugar, sifted

Preheat the oven to 325°F/160°C. Grease a shallow 9 inch/23 cm bundt pan or ring mold pan.

Sift the flour with the baking powder and a pinch of salt. Cream the butter and sugar until light and fluffy and pale in color. Add the eggs to the sugar mixture, beating them in one at a time, and adding a tablespoon of the flour with each one. Add the marmalade, caraway seeds, and the orange zest and juice, then fold in the remaining flour. Pour into the prepared pan.

Bake for about 45 minutes or until a skewer inserted into the cake comes out clean. Cool slightly before turning out. When cold, sprinkle the cake with confectioners' sugar.

MACAROONS

These classic macaroons are a favorite element of the "biscuit tin," often offered with a glass of sherry or a cup of tea.

edible rice paper
2 large egg whites
1 cup/110 g almond meal
almond or ratafia extract
generous 1 cup/225 g sugar
3 tablespoons/30 g rice flour
flaked almonds

Preheat the oven to 320°F/160°C and line two baking sheets with rice paper (or you can use parchment paper).

Lightly whisk the egg whites with a fork. Mix the almond meal, extract, sugar, and rice flour together. Mix in the whites thoroughly. Using a teaspoon, drop spoonfuls of the mixture onto the lined baking sheets, well apart, and top each one with an almond flake.

Bake until just golden brown, about 10–12 minutes. Transfer the macaroons, still on the paper, to a rack to cool. When cold, tear or cut away the excess rice paper from the edges of the cookies. The rice paper is, of course, edible.

WALNUT CAKE

3½ oz/100 g walnuts
1¾ sticks/200 g butter, at room temperature
generous ¾ cup/175 g sugar
4 large eggs, at room temperature
2 cups/280 g all-purpose flour, sifted
1 teaspoon vanilla extract
grated zest and juice of 1 small lemon

Preheat the oven to 350°F/180°C. Butter and line an 8 cup/900 g loaf pan (about 9 x 5 x 3 inches/23 x 13 x 8 cm).

Crumble the walnuts with your fingers. In a large bowl or mixer, cream the butter, then add the sugar, beating until pale and creamy. Add the eggs, one by one, adding a tablespoon of flour and beating well between each. Mix in the walnuts, vanilla, and 1 tablespoon lemon juice. Mix well, then fold in the remaining flour, in 3 parts, cutting it in rather than beating it, but making sure no flour pockets remain. Transfer the mixture to the prepared pan and sprinkle the top with lemon zest. Place a piece of foil loosely over the top.

Bake for about an hour, removing the foil and lowering the heat to 325°F/160°C after half an hour. Test with a skewer after 45 minutes. When cooked, cool for a few minutes in the pan before removing to a wire rack.

The cake can be iced with a little confectioners' sugar mixed with a tablespoon of lemon juice. It will keep for a few days in an airtight container.

Note: the walnuts can be toasted for 5 minutes in the oven for a nuttier flavor, but watch carefully because they burn quickly.

BARM BRACK

SERVES 6–8

"Barm" is the yeasty ferment produced when brewing ale or beer; "brack," or "breac," refers to its speckled nature. Barm brack is one of the few Irish traditional breads raised with yeast, and, like hot cross buns, the origins are lost in antiquity. It is an essential part of Irish Halloween festivities and, like colcannon, traditionally contains a small metal ring baked into the dough— as the custom goes, whoever gets the ring will be married within the year.

4–5 saffron strands

4 cups/560 g all-purpose flour

1 teaspoon salt

¼ cup/55 g brown sugar

2 teaspoons pumpkin pie spice, or to taste

½ oz/15 g envelope instant dry yeast

6 tablespoons/75 g butter

¾ lb/350 g mixed dried fruit and candied citrus peel

2 eggs, beaten

1¼ cups/300 ml warm milk

TO GLAZE

1 tablespoon sugar

Soak the saffron in 2 tablespoons water for 15 minutes.

In a large bowl, mix the flour, salt, sugar, spice, and yeast together. Rub in the butter and then add the dried fruit and candied citrus peel. Add the beaten eggs and the saffron mixture to the warm milk. Make a well in the flour mixture and pour in the liquid, reserving a tablespoon. Mix well together, drawing in the flour from the sides. When the mixture will hold together, turn it out and knead for 5–6 minutes. Return to the bowl and cover with plastic wrap. Allow to rise for about 1½ hours in a warm place.

Grease two 8 inch/20 cm cake pans. If you are adding the lucky rings, wrap them in wax paper. Turn the dough out and knead again briefly, then divide between the cake pans. Press the rings into the center and set aside to rise for a further 30 minutes.

Preheat the oven to 425°F/220°C. Brush the cakes with the reserved liquid and bake for about 10 minutes, then reduce the heat to 375°F/190°C and bake until a hollow sound results when the bottom is tapped, about 40–50 minutes. Make a glaze by boiling the sugar with ¼ cup water until it has reduced to a syrup. Brush this over the bracks and return to the oven to set for 5 minutes.

Note: if using, make sure your rings are heat-safe.

SODA BREAD WITH ONION

SERVES 6–8

This variation on classic Irish soda bread is especially good with pâté.

1 large onion, finely chopped
¼ cup/60 ml olive oil
3 cups/500 g white bread flour
½ teaspoon salt
1 teaspoon baking soda
2½ cups/600 ml buttermilk
2 teaspoons caraway seeds

Preheat the oven to 350°F/180°C and grease a baking sheet.

In a heavy pan, cook the onion in a tablespoon of the oil until dark brown and crisp but not burned. Cool.

Sift the flour and salt together. Dissolve the baking soda in 1 tablespoon of the buttermilk. Add this, with the remaining 3 tablespoons olive oil, to the rest of the buttermilk. Add the onions and seeds to the flour. Make a well in the center and add the liquid. With a fork, mix it all together thoroughly, mixing lightly until you have a fairly smooth texture, but don't knead.

With floured hands, shape the mixture into a round cake, cut a cross in the top, transfer to the baking sheet, and bake until the loaf gives a hollow sound when tapped on the bottom, about 40 minutes.

Note: if buttermilk is not available, use fresh milk and 2 teaspoons of baking powder.

PRESERVES

LOGANBERRY AND PLUM JAM

MAKES 2–3 X ½ PINT/8 OZ/225 G JARS OR FREEZER CONTAINERS

It seems more like fun to make small quantities of different jams with whatever is on hand, and this intensely flavored combination is well worth the half-hour it takes. If you can't find gooseberries, use more lemon juice.

½ lb/225 g plums
2 oz/55 g gooseberries
½ lb/225 g loganberries
2¼ cups/450 g sugar
1 tablespoon lemon juice

Simmer the plums and gooseberries in scant 1 cup/210 ml water until the plums are soft enough to remove the pits. Cut the plums in pieces, if they are large, and return them to the water. Add the loganberries, bring back to a boil, and cook for 5 minutes. Remove from the heat, pour in the sugar and lemon juice, and stir until completely dissolved.

Boil hard for 5–10 minutes until it sets when tested: Chill some saucers in the freezer and then test by putting a few drops of the mixture on a saucer and allowing to cool. If the surface of the drop wrinkles when pushed with a finger, the jam is ready. Pour into sterilized jars or clean freezer containers, allow to cool fully, and cover. Store in the freezer for up to 6 months or in the refrigerator for up to 3 weeks.

Note: This recipe has not been pH tested for further processing. Please refer to the USDA's National Center for Home Food Perservation website for more information on safe canning practices.

RASPBERRY JAM

MAKES 2 X 12 OZ/250 G JELLY JARS OR FREEZER CONTAINERS

The raspberry season is so short, but jams and preserves help to prolong the taste of summer.

3¼ cups/700 g sugar
1½ lb/700 g raspberries
¼ lb/110 g redcurrants
1 tablespoon lemon juice

Put the sugar into an ovenproof dish and warm gently in the oven.

Put the fruit in a stainless steel saucepan over a very low heat until the juice begins to flow, then bring very slowly to a boil and simmer for 10 minutes. Pour in the warmed sugar and lemon juice, and stir until the sugar has completely dissolved.

Boil hard until a few drops cooled on a chilled saucer will wrinkle when pushed with a finger (start testing after 6 minutes). Pour into in dry sterilized jars or clean freezer containers, allow to cool fully, and seal. Store in the freezer for up to 6 months or in the refrigerator for up to 3 weeks.

Note: This recipe has not been pH tested for further processing. Please refer to the USDA's National Center for Home Food Perservation website for more information on safe canning practices.

Overleaf: Slea Head and Coumeenoole Beach.

ROSE-PETAL VINEGAR

SERVES 6

Use this delicate vinegar to flavor summer salads, or try a few drops on summer fruits, such as strawberries and raspberries; it seems to bring out the flavors. The choice of the base vinegar is important. Use a good-quality white-wine vinegar, or organic cider vinegar. Rice vinegar, which can be bought from Asian grocery stores and most supermarkets, is particularly delicate in flavor.

Measure equal quantities of vinegar and scented rose petals, about 2 large cupfuls of each. Put them together in a glass container and cover tightly. They should be left to steep on a sunny window for at least 3 weeks. If you like a stronger flavor, strain off the petals and add fresh ones, then steep a little longer. Strain into bottles and cork tightly. Elderflower vinegar can be made the same way.

Below: Glandore Village.

CHRISTMAS CHUTNEY

MAKES ABOUT 2 X 12 OZ/350 G JARS OR FREEZER CONTAINERS

1 lb/450 g Bramley or other tart cooking apples

1 medium/175 g onion, finely chopped

⅔ cup/150 ml white-wine vinegar

½ cup/112 g white sugar

2 tablespoons/40 g brown sugar

¼ lb/112 g mixed nuts, e.g. chestnuts, walnuts, and almonds

1 teaspoon ground ginger

grated zest and juice of ½ lemon

½ teaspoon salt

Peel, core, and chop the apples. Cook the onions in the vinegar until soft. Add the apples, cook for 3–4 minutes, and then add the remaining ingredients. Simmer gently until the mixture begins to thicken, lowering the heat and stirring frequently to prevent it from burning.

Spoon the mixture into sterilized jars or clean freezer containers, allow to cool fully, and cover. Store in the freezer for up to 6 months or in the refrigerator for up to 3 weeks.

Note: This recipe has not been pH tested for further processing. Please refer to the USDA's National Center for Home Food Perservation website for information on safe canning practices.

ROWAN BERRY JELLY

MAKES 3 X 12 OZ/350 G JARS OR FREEZER CONTAINERS

The rowan tree, or mountain ash, like the elder tree, had important magical properties for our Celtic ancestors. The red berries make an excellent jelly for game, hams, and pâtés, the flavor maturing as it ages. Rowan berry jelly can be used instead of redcurrant jelly in sauces and with lamb. Look for them in farmers' markets or your neighbor's yard!

1½ lb/700 g rowan berries

1 large Bramley or other tart cooking apple,
    coarsely chopped

grated zest and juice of 1 lemon

granulated sugar

Put the rowan berries in a large saucepan and crush them slightly. Add the coarsely chopped apples (no need to peel or core), and lemon zest. Just cover with water and cook until both are very soft.

Strain overnight, through a jelly bag (or use an old linen dish towel over a large plastic colander). Be careful not to squeeze the bag—it must drip naturally, or the jelly will be cloudy.

Measure the juice collected, add the lemon juice, and add 1¼ cups/225g sugar for every 1¼ cups/300 ml liquid. Boil hard until a few drops on a chilled saucer will wrinkle when pressed with a finger. Pour into sterilized jars or clean freezer containers, allow to cool, and seal tightly. Store in the freezer for up to 6 months or in the refrigerator for up to 3 weeks.

Note: This recipe has not been pH tested for further processing. Please refer to the USDA's National Center for Home Food Perservation website for information on safe canning practices.

Overleaf: Sea inlet mountains, Dingle Peninsula, County Kerry.

Acknowledgments

I would like to thank Christine Cullen for her generous assistance in preparing the manuscript and her helpful suggestions throughout the work. I'd also like to thank Eveleen Coyle and Fleur Robertson for the idea and for their confidence and patience, and my cooking friends and colleagues for inspiration.

First American edition published in 2015 by

INTERLINK BOOKS

An imprint of Interlink Publishing Group, Inc.
46 Crosby Street
Northampton, Massachusetts 01060
www.interlinkbooks.com

Library of Congress Cataloging-in-Publication Data available

ISBN 978-1-56656-095-5

10 9 8 7 6 5 4 3 2 1
Printed and bound in China

Editors: Fleur Robertson and Emily Preece-Morrison
American edition editor: Leyla Moushabeck
Home economy: Valerie Berry
Styling: Davina Perkins
Recipe photography: Tony Briscoe
Landscape photography: Michael Diggin Photography
Cover design: Julian D. Ramirez